Appsters

A Beginner's Guide to App Entrepreneurship

BOBBY GILL

JORDAN GURRIERI

For Golgi and his apparatus

CONTENTS

1.

Introduction

You might not know it, but they are all around us. Samuel L. Jackson is one of them, and so too are Jimmy Fallon and Chuck Norris. From the guy wearing the tight jeans and thick-rimmed glasses furiously tapping away on his Mac, to the Mom comforting her crying toddler with her iPhone, Appsters come in all sorts of shapes, sizes and colors. They look just like you and me, and you'd be hard pressed to identify an Appster until they ask you to try their app. If you've ever looked down at your phone and wondered to yourself, "I wish there was an app that...," then you too have a little Appster inside of you waiting to be unleashed.

In the common tongue, an Appster is someone who has created their own mobile app. Being an Appster isn't predicated on you knowing how to program your own app. In fact, there are many who have no technical experience whatsoever. Being an Appster means taking the risk and setting off into the unknown to turn your idea into a real app. Appsters are entrepreneurs who have built businesses on the bleeding edge of technology with their own mobile apps.

You aren't alone in this journey; thousands of people have taken the plunge before you and emerged an Appster. You, too, will face many of the same challenges and obstacles that they've overcome. The path to Appsterdom is well worn, but it's hard to find if you've never gone down this road before. We've written this book to guide you along, from just having an idea clanging around in your head to becoming an Appster with your own app business.

With this book, you'll learn what it takes to build a business based on a mobile app. From breaking down the economics of the app world to choosing a mobile platform, all the way down designing mobile user interfaces, we're going to equip you with the knowledge and understanding you'll need to go from being just another person with an idea for a mobile app to someone who has a mobile app business.

The road from idea to Appster is neither short nor easy. We can't tell you that your app will be the next DrawSomething or that your app company will be bought out for millions by Facebook. For those types of prognostications, you should see a psychic. What we do know is that launching a mobile app is tough and that those who do achieve astronomical success in the app arena are both a product of their own brilliance and of that great lady named Luck.

For every app like Instagram or Path, there are thousands of other apps that sit in obscurity on the app store. Some of these apps, like Forecast, will quietly disappear without any of the press or hype that surrounded their launch. But others, the countless thousands of little fish in the vast waters of the app store, are joined each day by thousands of new apps, all of which are jockeying to define themselves within the rapidly growing mobile applications market.

Contrary to what the Twitterverse might proclaim or what you've read on TechCrunch, you can be a successful Appster without being featured on the cover of BusinessWeek or receiving an offer sheet from Facebook. The world of mobile apps is like an iceberg jutting out from the sea. Below the surface, beneath the conversations and press releases, is a vast technological frontier - one that it is experiencing exponential growth and usurping the entire personal computing industry. You won't hear about the simple, non-disruptive apps that quietly churn out thousands of dollars of revenue each month to their creators. You won't hear about the stories of people with no technical training or programming knowledge, but who had the right amount of analytical skill and awareness to take their app from abstract idea to a revenue producing reality.

The odds that any one mobile app will reach pop-culture notoriety are slim, but those who succeed in mobile apps aren't betting on it. Each day, with every new app released, Appsters are accumulating wealth $0.99 at a time. $0.99 is the price most apps sell for, and after all is said and done, only about $0.70 lands in an Appster's pockets. Yet, you'd be myopic to dismiss its potential by such a small amount of money: the mobile app world is a rapidly growing landscape with over 1 million smartphones activated and over $15 million dollars spent on in-app purchases each day.[1]

If you can create an app that is able to carve out some small tiny fraction of this landscape, suddenly $0.70 per sale starts to add up to real money. No, we don't know how to build the next global app phenomenon, but we do know that there's more than enough money clanging around in the niches of the app market to free you from the 9-5 grind.

Achieving success as an Appster requires many things, but being a programmer is not one of them. Building a great mobile app is more a product of understanding human emotion than one of deep programming knowledge. Ask most software engineers and they'll tell you that while programming mobile apps poses unique challenges, it is for the most part a technically straightforward exercise. This doesn't mean you should head to your local Barnes & Noble and pick up a copy of *Mobile App Programming for Dummies*. If you don't know how to program, don't try to become a programmer. It won't work. Programming is but one step in a release cycle that requires creativity, leadership, pragmatism and knowledge.

If you have a mobile app idea bouncing around in your head, one that won't let you sleep and agitates you to take action, then this book is for you. If you have the business acumen and market savvy to identify an opportunity in the app marketplace, but not the technical skills to build an app to fill it, then this book is for you.

We've written this book to be a pocket guide to launching a mobile app business. Over the course of this book, you will find the advice, guidance and methodologies that will empower you to go from just having an idea about a mobile app to having a real app in just a few weeks.

Within this book, we'll share lessons and experience from ourselves along with a host of other Appsters about the key ingredients to creating a mobile app. We'll start at the very highest level in examining the mobile app landscape and explore what separates a good mobile app from the rest of the pack. Part of this exercise is learning both the usability and design aspect, as well as the financial realities of app entrepreneurship. We'll explore the various ways apps can generate revenue, along with an exploration of the costs associated with developing a mobile application.

From there, we'll do a technical overview where we'll untangle the jumbled mass of acronyms and technical jargon and give you a solid understanding of what technical components make up a mobile app, along with an understanding how each acronym fits into the overall picture. We don't intend to make you a programmer, but we'll give you the confidence to engage everybody from a VC to an engineer in technical conversations. After that, we'll give you a tutorial on how to best manage your engineering effort and give you well-worn knowledge on how to navigate the minefield that is software engineering.

Since getting your app built is only the first step, we'll spend the last part of the book exploring how to get users to use your app and what makes a great mobile app marketing strategy.

By the end of this book, we will have equipped you with the knowledge to take the next step and embark on the road to Appsterdom.

1.1

Meet Our Sample App: 'Dani's List'

Our goal is to guide you go through the app development process, from idea to app. To reinforce the lessons of this text, we'll be building up our very own sample app as we move through the book. By doing this, we hope to frame the lessons of each chapter in the context of creating a real app.

The app we will be building is called 'Dani's List'. The idea behind it is simple: provide an easy way for people to create and share fun things to do with those around them. With Dani's List, the aim is to create an app that lets people manage their own 'what to do list' of activities populated with their own ideas and those created by other users of the app. With Dani's List, a user can open the app and see their own list of things they want to do, as well as browse ideas that other people have added to their own lists. The activities people create can be anything, from going to a place to eat to going to the park and flying a kite. When people complete an activity, they can mark them complete and move on to the next item on their 'what to do list'.

While Dani's List might not sound like an Earth-shattering idea, it is a great example of the types of apps that people are creating today. It combines personal utility, social networking and location-based discovery. As we move through the book, we'll apply lessons we learn to develop the Dani's List app.

You can follow along at home by downloading the Dani's List app, available for free on the Apple App Store.

2.

Welcome to the Appverse

We never thought technology would ever be considered sexy, especially after that minor debacle known as the *dot-com crash*. From *big data*, the eponymous *cloud*, to the *mobile apps* revolution, people have gone gaga for technology. We are surprised at this turn of events not because we doubted the power of technology, but because we never imagined the day when it would emerge from the shadows of the 'techie' world to become the next big gold rush for anyone with an idea and some determination.

Today, it sometimes seems like everybody and his or her great-uncle has an idea for a mobile app. Be it one that changes the channel of your TV, to one that gives you the location of the nearest public restroom, app ideas are in full dot-com bloom.

Given you are reading this book, you probably have an idea for an app that you want to build. And you are not alone. There are over 700,000[6] apps on Apple's App Store and 600 more are added each day. While creating software written for PCs and Macs was strictly the realm of the technologically adept, the App Store has over 170,000 active app publishers and has made Appsters of everyone from stay at home moms to celebrities and even a few politicians.

The allure of mobile apps is hard to deny, even with today's frothy hype that might become tomorrow's full-fledged bubble. Even with the exponential adoption curve of mobile devices and the rapidly evolving app landscape, we are still at the beginning of what has been called the *post-PC era* of computing. While the mobile handset market has matured, other form factors, like the tablet, have only recently gained attention, with others, like the TV, having yet to have their own iPhone moment. As computing spreads around the house, the concept of the *app* will remain a conceptual foundation for how people interact with their data and the Internet in the post-PC era.

2.1

The 'Post-PC Era'

We are in the midst of a great transformation in personal computing: we are entering what Steve Jobs once called the *post-PC era*[2]. Mobile applications are at the vanguard of a movement away from traditional laptop and desktop computer interfaces towards more pervasive mediums such as cell phones, TVs and appliances. Instead of sitting stationary in front of a computer, the post-PC era is marked by the ability to stay connected at all times using *smart devices* which provide internet connectivity and much of the functionality as a regular laptop computer. The emergence of smartphones represents the first jump away from the keyboard and mouse that have marked computing for the past 30 years. Smartphones were the first wave of devices to threaten the dominance of the traditional computer, with other form factors such as Tablets and Smart TVs emerging as the second and third waves of the post-PC revolution.

The shift towards smart devices in lieu of PCs has come about because of the continued advancement of microchip and battery technology, along with the maturation of Internet-based *cloud* services. Perhaps the most abused of all modern tech monikers, the cloud within the consumer space means having your data available to you wherever you are. Instead of storing your documents, pictures and videos on the hard drive of a computer, the cloud enables you to store them on 3rd party services that are accessible from any Internetconnected device. Notable cloud services include Google's Gmail, Microsoft Office 365, Dropbox, and Evernote. The availability of high-capacity, low-cost storage in the cloud enabled the proliferation of smart phones as it reduced the need to for large-capacity hard drives that are only available on traditional PCs. With the cloud, a user can move through their day, from device to device, without ever being disconnected from their data.

History Lesson: The Story so Far

In only the past 5 years, the post-PC movement, with mobile apps and the cloud at the forefront, has grown into a global revolution that has disrupted the entire computing industry and opened a gold rush upon the mobile frontier. To understand what makes a mobile app different, we must first understand where we came from. If you would be so kind to accompany us down a trip through memory lane, let's look at what personal computing meant just 5 years ago in the world of 2007:

Back in those olden days, using the Internet meant sitting at a keyboard, staring into a screen while using a mouse to click your way through the Web. Now, to give 2007 some credit, we had laptops and wireless Internet, so it wasn't like we were living the Dark Ages. However, as anyone who's ever tried using a laptop while walking around will attest, we were chained to our computers. The cellular phone was the obvious next step for computing, yet all attempts at making a cellular phone an Internet-enabled device floundered as manufacturers held onto the keyboard and mouse pointer metaphor.

For the few of us who had smartphones, they were either in the form of a Windows Mobile phone that was a PC interface disguised in a tiny, tiny package, or a Blackberry that provided exceptional thumb typing ability, but did nothing to change the interaction of model of a computer. Everybody else? Well they were probably on a Motorola Razr, a T-Mobile Sidekick or some LG/Samsung/Sony flip phone that were Internet-enabled only in name.

The Blackberry and Windows Mobile smartphones were great email devices, but they were stunted as Internet devices by tiny screens and crippled Internet browsers that required web sites to be built on a brittle specification called the Wireless Application Protocol (WAP) in order for them to be viewable from a smartphone.

While the concept of mobile applications did exist on these early smartphones, there was no notion of a centralized marketplace to purchase them, let alone a simple, one-click process to add and remove them from the phone. (Ever tried installing an app on a Windows Mobile 6.0 phone? Good luck with that.)

Mobile computing was stuck. Everybody knew mobile was the

future, however nobody had cracked the code to make it mainstream. The established giants in the smartphone market couldn't break free of the metaphor provided by the mouse and keyboard. The closest we had to mobile innovation was a weird, bastard-child of a laptop called a "Netbook", which was an underpowered laptop with a tiny keyboard that ran Windows XP.

Then, in the spring of 2007 came Apple's iPhone and iOS operating system. With its large touch screen and tap/swipe/pinch interface, the iPhone heralded a new age of personal computing that broke cleanly away from the notion of mouse and keyboard.

The beauty of the iPhone was not that it had the best battery life (it was terrible and couldn't be replaced) or the fastest connection (it didn't have 3G), but that it made most of the Internet accessible with a single hand. You couldn't do much beyond the basic set of apps that shipped with the iPhone, but you could do all of it while walking down Manhattan's 34th street in rush hour. The Safari browser on the iPhone rendered most web sites like they appeared on a laptop, which, combined with the pinch/tap finger gestures to zoom and move across a page, finally gave people the ability to interact with the same Internet they used on a laptop.

The first iPhone laid the foundation for the emergence of the *app*. With the introduction of the iPhone 3G in 2008, Apple allowed independent software developers to create their own apps for the iPhone and distribute them via the Apple App Store. The App Store by then had become the defacto standard for people to purchase and manage music on the iPod music player. By integrating apps as another item to be purchased and managed through the App Store interface, Apple immediately created a vibrant marketplace with an established set of customers for the purchasing of mobile apps for the iPhone 3Gs. Almost immediately the mobile app craze began, with a torrent of apps appearing on the App Store that allowed people to do anything from answer the age old question of *What song is playing right now?* with the Shazam app, to generating fart noises on-demand with a touch using the iFart app.

The allure of mobile apps captivated the world, as evidenced by the cultural adoption of Apple's pitch line, *There's an app for that*. The popularity of the concept of the app was driven both by the simple abstraction it provided to the end user along with the seamless, low-cost model of purchasing new apps provided by the App Store. On the iPhone, a mobile app could be downloaded with one tap and begin functioning right away. There was no separate *install* process that was common in the PC/Mac world, as the concept of the app encapsulated all functionality and requirements needed for it to run. Users could install new apps with a single tap and just as easily remove them when they were done.

Further, the Apple App Store brought the $0.99 model that Apple had pioneered with music to software. The App Store created a land-rush for software developers to bring their own apps to market as people's insatiable demand and willingness to pay $0.99 for even the most basic app brought dollar signs to their eyes. While the price of the software had fallen, the customer base provided by the App Store enabled app developers to generate revenue by the sheer number of potential customers at their doorstep.

The iPhone was a runaway hit and propelled the resurgent Apple to become the world's most valuable company in 2011. The popularity of the iPhone broke the logjam that was mobile computing with the entire industry making a shift towards the touch-enabled, app-centric devices.

Google soon followed Apple and released its own mobile operating system named *Android* in 2008. Like the iPhone, Android was designed to support a touch interface and provided a centralized marketplace called Google Play for users of the Android operating system to purchase new apps. Unlike the iPhone, which was an operating system plus hardware bundled as one, Google created Android as a universal operating system standard that could run on a multitude of devices manufactured by any smartphone maker. (For those of you that remember the early days of the PC, the strategy that Google pursued with Android is very similar to that which Microsoft pioneered with MS/DOS and Windows.) App developers could create mobile apps for the Android operating system and, through the Google Play marketplace, have them be available to almost any user on any phone running the Android operating system.

If iPhone broke the logjam, then Android unleashed a torrent of smartphones into the consumer marketplace. In the four years since it was released, the Android operating system now powers over 400 million smart devices.[3]

However, smartphones were just the first step, and in 2010, Apple further blurred the line between a computer and device with the introduction of the iPad tablet. Essentially a large screened iPhone, the iPad directly challenged the dominance of laptops as it provided much the same functionality of the iPhone with the added benefit of a larger screen. Very soon after its release, consumers began purchasing iPads in lieu of a new laptop, and the tablet became synonymous with casual Internet browsing. Android wasn't far behind and soon announced support for tablet form factor devices such as the Samsung Galaxy Tab and Motorola XOOM tablet.

While the iPhone turned the cellular phone industry on its head, the iPad took direct aim at the notion of a laptop computer. The success of the iPhone and iPad has been so meteoric that Apple's iPhone/iPad business by itself is more profitable than all of Microsoft[4]. While the PC's hold on the business market remains firm, the rapid proliferation of smartphones, tablets, and other smart devices has heralded the dawn of the post-PC era.

Platform	Market share % (July 2012)
Google Android	52%
Apple iOS	33%
RIM Blackberry	10%
Microsoft Windows Phone	4%

Figure 1: Mobile Market share by platform as of July 2012[5]

2.2

Meet the Mobile App

A mobile app is an evolution of what we normally would call an *application* on a PC or Mac. To any user of a modern smartphone, they'd know a mobile app to be one of those small rectangular icons that dot a smartphone's screen. However, the term mobile app is an overloaded one, as it can mean two different things depending on whom you ask.

When you hear of a mobile app, you are likely envisioning one that you download to your phone via a marketplace like Apple's App Store. Apps like these are called *native apps*, because they live on your phone and run directly atop your smartphone's operating system. Native apps are written specifically to run on a particular smartphone platform like Apple's iOS or Google Android. Native apps cannot run on different platforms without being completely written in the programming language of that platform.

However, there exists another type of app: a *mobile web app* that lives within the smartphone browser that brings the power of web development to the mobile phone and enables them to be used on any modern smartphone.

Figure 2: Mobile Web App (left) vs. Native App (right)

Mobile Web Apps

An alternative to native apps is the concept of *mobile web apps*, which run within a smartphone web browser. You might have heard mobile web apps being referred to as *HTML5 apps*. A mobile web app is just a web site that has been styled to fit the smaller screen of a smartphone. Just like regular web sites face restrictions as to what they can or cannot do to a person's computer, so do mobile web apps. However, with the advent of HTML5, the latest version of the venerable web browsing standard, mobile web apps can be built to replicate much of what previously could only be achieved with a native app.

The great advantage of mobile web apps is platform independence, as they can be used on any device with a modern web browser regardless of what mobile platform its running. Native apps on the other hand are explicitly developed with only 1 target platform in mind. Additionally, if you have an existing web site and are looking to create a mobile experience based on it, then the mobile web app route is very appealing as the effort to modify an existing web app for a mobile browser is much less than it is to write a native app from scratch.

Still, mobile web apps have limitations because they run within a web browser, and not directly on the smartphone's operating system. If you want your app to receive push notifications, use location services, or use the phone's camera, a mobile web app will typically not work. In general, mobile web apps are great for experiences that are consumptive in nature, like a cookbook or restaurant review app, but do not work for apps that require access to the smartphone hardware, such asInstagram or Spotify.

The popularity of mobile web apps has recently taken a hit by Facebook's decision to switch from apps largely built on HTML to those built on native app technology. In previous' versions of the Facebook mobile apps, users constantly complained about poor responsiveness of the user interface (UI) and the speed of the app, both of which were limitations brought on by mobile web app technology. In 2012, Facebook ditched the HTML5 based apps and moved to native apps as they offered the speed and responsiveness that couldn't be delivered by the mobile web app version. We'll talk more about how to choose between building a mobile web app and a native app a little bit later on in this book.

Native Apps

Native apps on a smartphone are similar to the concept of an application on a PC, though native apps differ in that they operate within a much more restrictive environment than a PC/Mac application. Mobile apps simplify the abstract concepts of an application away from the user by eliminating much of the customizability and complexity that traditional desktop applications provide.

For example, in Windows, an application usually comes with its own installer that can be programmed by the developer to ask the user any number of questions so that the software can be configured precisely to the user's needs. Mobile apps forego this entire installer component and are all installed in the same one-click manner from a marketplace. The benefit to this is that the potentially confusing process of running a *setup* program is completely avoided at the expense of enhanced customizability of the app.

Another difference between a native app and a traditional PC/Mac application is that on a Windows or Mac computer, applications operate alongside each other as tenants of the host operating system that can share data with each other. On the other hand, mobile apps operate in a more silo-ed fashion where apps operate independently from one another.

For instance, on a Mac, applications can store and share data with each other on the file system by using the concept of a *file* (e.g., you save a text file in Text Edit, you can open it up in Word). Mobile apps are completely self-contained - they manage their own data as they see fit with no concept of a *file* or *folder* being exposed to the user for sharing data between apps. You'll come to find that many of the complexities of traditional applications, such as managing registry settings and sharing of files (what we used to call 'DLL hell'), don't exist in mobile apps precisely because there is no overarching need to enable apps to talk to each other.

Furthermore, viruses and malware become much less of an issue with mobile apps since they operate in much more regulated environment than in Windows or a Mac.

Finally, traditional PC/Mac applications, once launched, operate autonomously with little to no interference from the operating system. They continue to be active so long as the user does not explicitly close them. With mobile apps, the lifecycle of an app is much more actively managed by the smartphone operating system. For instance, when you launch an app on the iPhone, the operating system instructs the program to commence executing. However, if you press the button to return to the home screen, the operating system instructs the application to move into a *sleep* state. If you then return to the app, the operating system instructs the sleeping application to reawaken and resume execution. If you don't return to the app in a timely fashion, the operating system may choose to *kill* the app and close it. Contrast this with traditional applications where the user is given more direct control over the lifecycle of an application and chooses when the application should quit.

The most obvious difference between traditional PC/Mac applications and native mobile apps is the way people interact with them. On a Mac or PC, you'd use a keyboard and mouse to interact with a program. On the other hand, a mobile app is *touch-enabled*, which is a fancy way of saying people control them with their fingers. While this might seem like a minor difference, the absence of the mouse and keyboard completely change how applications are designed for mobile phones. We'll explore some of things to remember when designing for mobile a little later in the book.

If you take one lesson from this entire section, it's that the notion of a mobile app is just a more abstract concept of a traditional desktop application, with much of the latter's customization sacrificed in the name of simplicity. As an aspiring Appster, this might seem stifling and limiting, but simplicity is at the heart of what has made the concept of a mobile app so successful.

2.3

The Marketplace

Part of the success of the native app is due to the availability of high-quality apps through centralized marketplaces like the Apple App Store and Google Play. Apps can only be installed on a smartphone through that smartphone's app marketplace.

But you can't just create any old app and put it for sale on the App Store. It needs to be approved by Apple before it can be listed in the marketplace. This approval process is designed to ensure that only high-quality apps are ever installed on a user's phone, filtering out the noise of poorly built apps and malicious viruses. For consumers, the tight control Apple holds over the listing in the App Store is a boon, as the chances of downloading an app that turns out to be spyware is rare. As an app developer, the restrictions on apps that Apple places in order to be listed in App Store can be stifling.

On the other hand, Android's marketplace, Google Play, is much less restrictive and requires little to no approval for submitting new apps. We'll cover more about app marketplaces in a later chapter, but know for now that your path to releasing a native app requires navigating an app store approval process, and that the app store is going to take some of your revenue (usually 30%). We know it's not fair, but like Run DMC said, that's just the way it is.

2.4

An App for Every Season: The Different Types of Apps

The app landscape is big. And we mean really big! As of mid-2013, there were over 800,000 apps on the Apple App Store, and similarly 800,000 on the Google Play marketplace[6]. With those kinds of numbers, it's easy to know that not all apps are created equal. Like Baskin Robbins ice cream, apps come in all sorts of varieties and flavors: from single player card games to those that fling birds across the screen; from apps that let you message your friends to apps that let you make fun of people with your friends; from task management tools to virtual notebooks; the imaginations of Appsters and their resulting creations knows no bounds.

In general, you can bucket apps into one of the following five categories: Gaming, Social Networking, Informational, Communication, and Utility.

Figure 3: The app landscape can be summarized by the intersection of 5 simple categories

Gaming

Apps like 'Angry Birds', 'Temple Run', 'FIFA Soccer', 'Farmville', etc. can be neatly classified as Games. As the name implies, these apps usually contain immersive video and audio experiences designed to entertain the user like a traditional video game. However, unlike an Xbox or PlayStation, gaming apps have much more simplified controls that rely entirely on touch and swipe gestures. Further, like the Nintendo Wii, many gaming apps use the position and movement of the phone as an additional control input, such that a player can handle the phone like a steering wheel when playing 'NASCAR'. Gaming apps tend to rely heavily on the 3D graphics processing capabilities of the phone and come with user interfaces that are custom designed and rendered by the app itself. Gaming apps tend to be resource intensive, both in terms memory and CPU time, but more importantly, battery life.

Social Networking

Social networking apps are the mobile manifestation of websites like Facebook, Instagram, Foursquare and Pinterest. Like their desktop counterparts, social networking apps enable users to view updates posted through their social networks in addition to updating them with photos, videos and text taken from the smartphone. Social networking apps go far beyond what you'd use on a laptop and often leverage the phone's location functionality to connect with people physically near the device.In particular, apps such as Highlight and Grindr have pushed the social networking frontier forward by giving people the ability to use their phone to meet and interact with the people right around them. In general, dedicated social networking apps are less resource intensive than gaming apps as they tend to have very simple user interfaces, with the major source of battery impact coming from the use of location services.

In the mobile app-verse, social networking can also be viewed as a cross-cutting capability that has introduced social functionality to other app categories. App such as Path, Quora, and GroupMe are all apps that fall into other categories, but also include social networking functionality. Thus, you can look at social networking as a capability that can be introduced to almost any type for app.

Informational

Apps that fall into this category are used to consume news, books, weather and other media on a smartphone. Notable examples of informational apps are Flipboard, the New York Times, Kindle, Pulse and Instapaper apps. Informational apps are generally very lightweight, as they don't do much beyond render content to the reader. The straightforward nature of these apps lends them particularly well to be developed as mobile web apps instead of natively written ones.

Fun fact: In 2011, due to a dispute with Apple, the Financial Times pulled down its natively written iPhone app and replaced it with a mobile web app that was accessible via the Safari browser. In a blow to Apple, the Financial Times decided to do this after Apple refused to let the FT process its own in-app subscriptions outside of the App Store[7]. We'll talk more about the financial aspects of selling on the app marketplaces a little later in the book.

Informational apps have had their greatest impact on tablet devices. The tablet's larger screen makes them perfectly suited for reading newspapers, watching videos and viewing pictures. The power of tablets for consuming traditional media has been a large source of disruption for struggling newspaper and magazine publishers. Apps like Instapaper and Pulse create beautiful consumptive experiences on the tablet that leave traditional newspaper and magazine web sites trailing far behind. To stake a foothold in the race to bring news and other content to the tablet form factor, media giants like News Corporation have embraced this trend by releasing their own tablet-only newspapers, such as The Daily.

Communication

As you would expect from the name, communication apps enable people to send text, audio and video messages to each other using the Internet. The great benefit of these types of apps is that the cellular carriers do not bill their usage. Since communication apps run over the Internet, carriers are unable to toll them like traditional SMS messages. In addition to mobile upstarts like GroupMe and WhatsApp, the communication space is also home more established services such as Microsoft's Skype and Apple's iMessage.

The great threat faced by app creators in the communication space is encroachment of their functionality by both hardware manufacturers and the mobile platforms themselves. With the release of IOS 5.0, Apple introduced iMessage, a feature on the iPhone that allowed iPhone users to send messages to each other over the Internet, much like WhatsApp and GroupMe do. As mobile platform makers gradually include more functionality like iMessage into the smartphones themselves, the need for separate messaging apps is likely to shrink. This places apps like WhatsApp into a difficult long-term position as their core value proposition is eroded by platform capabilities. Be it the cellular carriers or the mobile platform makers themselves, it is likely that as the mobile platforms mature, more and more instant-communication functionality will be built into the platform, thus shrinking the available real estate for independently developed communication apps.

Utility

Utility apps are straightforward to understand: they provide functionality to help solve specific needs of their users. Utility apps provide tangible value to their customers, and as such are much better positioned to generate revenue through app sales on the marketplace. Examples of utility apps are: Remember-the-Milk, Evernote, Fandango, Yelp, Urbanspoon and our very own Dani's List. Each of these apps is designed to provide their user with the capability or knowledge to fill a day-to-day need. Utility apps aren't the sexiest type of app, but from a pure monetization standpoint, building an app that solves a specific customer need is the best way to potentially generate revenue from sales of an app.

3.

'So I have this idea for an app…'

Before you run off proclaiming yourself to be the next Steve Jobs, be warned: mobile app ideas are a dime a dozen. Your idea is just an abstract thought in your head, a *wouldn't it be cool if…* Ideas are not the secret sauce to your success - your ability to execute and deliver product is much more important. The great challenge of mobile application development is not coming up with a unique problem to solve, but rather delivering an experience that resonates with your users and leaves them wanting more. The App Store is filled with great ideas, but as any app developer will tell you, great ideas do not necessarily make great apps.

Having a great idea for an app is a good start, but creating a great product is what will define your trajectory. The explosion of apps, combined with the fast-paced, connected society we live in, has made building apps more of an exercise in understanding human interaction patterns and emotion, and less to do with disruptive innovation. Not only does your app have to be interesting enough for someone to try it, but it also only has about 10 seconds to leave enough of an impression on the user that they would come back to use it again in the future. Great ideas that are poorly executed through non-intuitive design, over-complexity or poor engineering might get downloaded once, but they probably won't ever be used again.

Great apps emerge from regular, often-tried ideas that, through a mixture of intuitive design, addictive flow and viral marketing, snowball into runaway hits. The great apps aren't the ones that break a new technology barrier or introduce a new paradigm for communication. The great apps are the ones that connect with their audience and leave them wanting more. Great apps understand the contexts in which users will use it, and deliver experiences designed for them.

Building a great mobile app is more art than engineering and requires far more iteration than building a website or desktop app. Most app projects we've been a part of started with one idea and gradually morphed into something far different. One of the first apps we worked on started out as a location-based dating service. However, through 3 or 4 revisions, the idea slowly morphed into something completely different: a photo-captioning game. While creating a detailed specification and UI mock-ups helps guide the development process, they are no substitute for watching someone actually interact with your app. The first time somebody who isn't you or your engineering team picks up your app and tries it, you'll see things your spec never covered or even had completely wrong. The emotional element of mobile apps is difficult to specify beforehand and the only way to refine it is by watching people use your app.

Modern development methodologies, like *lean* and *agile*, stress a highly iterative process punctuated by frequent releases to customers, which holds true in mobile app development. Apps don't roll off a production line ready to shoot up the App Store sales charts; instead, they evolve into a final form after many rounds of iteration. Quite often, the app ends up being far different in look and functionality than originally envisioned. Expect and embrace change during the app development process. Your idea is just the starting point on a long journey to the final product.

Your idea, no matter how cool and disruptive your friends tell you it is, is worth nothing more than the paper it is written on. With over 800,000 apps on the Apple App Store, you should expect that somebody else has already come up with it and has even tried to build it. We tell you this not to dishearten or demotivate you from your quest, but rather to remind you that the failure of others is a great opportunity for you to learn and improve your own app. Your idea is just a starting point, a seed of invention that will remain precisely that unless you water it with user feedback and give it the time it needs to grow.

The hardest part of product development is not finding the right problem to solve, but building a product that engages its users and develops a following of its own. The most spectacular PowerPoint presentation will never provide you with this insight, and spending time developing slides over developing product is as much a waste of time as the space it wastes on your computer's hard disk. Even if you are only able to build a prototype that is nothing more than a non-functional UI, you'll learn about your users and how they think about your problem in ways that go far beyond anything you could imagine in a written specification.

3.1

The Ten Appster Commandments

Building a great mobile app is not easy, even for those experienced with building web sites and desktop applications. While the code underlying a mobile app is similar in structure and operation to traditional software, the way people interact with mobile apps is completely different and comes with its own unique set of challenges. As we move through this book, we'll try to point out these pitfalls and give you guidance on best practices developed by other mobile entrepreneurs. For now, we want you to always keep in mind a basic set of principles, commandments if you will, of mobile app development. If this is your first time building an app, then you should print these out and pin them in front of you somewhere.

1. Great ideas do not make great apps.

2. Your idea **will** change.

3. Ideas are worth nothing without a product. Focus on delivering product.

4. Release schedules will slip, be prepared and ready to adapt.

5. Release early and often, avoid development milestones longer than 6 weeks.

6. Share your idea with anyone willing to listen.

7. Watch how people use your app, see how they react and interact with it.

8. Functional specifications should not be treated as gospel. They become outdated the moment development begins.

9. You get what you pay for when hiring designers and engineers.

10. Don't be afraid to pivot. Fail early, learn, adjust and try again.

Figure 4: The 10 Appster Commandments

3.2

What Makes a Great App?

In case you are expecting a concrete answer, don't hold your breath. We don't have one. We don't know the recipe for making a smash hit app, much like movie producers can't tell you how to make a blockbuster movie.

When you identify a problem for your app to solve, that gives you a starting point in the app process. That's the easy part. With mobile apps, people are quick to label an idea great because the idea might be interesting, novel or solves a legitimate need, yet that doesn't necessarily yield a great app.

It's relatively easy to identify what makes a bad app: poor engineering, awkward user interfaces and uninspired content are just a few. The other side of the coin, the factors that make apps great are much harder to pinpoint. From what we've seen, and from what other Appsters will tell you, great apps tend to combine interesting ideas with sound engineering, fluid user experiences and strong emotional connections with their users. But that's not all; great apps are built to broadcast themselves and are designed for viral spread, if and when they do. From our experience building apps, along with interviews with other mobile entrepreneurs, here are some common ingredients that many great apps share:

Reason #1: They Deliver Great User Experiences

The user experience of an app goes beyond the colors and layout of its UI. It describes how users interact with the app. When you think about the user experience of an app, you should step back from any particular set of functionality and think about the broader contexts in which people will use your app. Are people likely to use your app at work or at home? Is your app meant to be an on-the-go app, or more for sitting back and killing time? Will people look to use your app for entertainment or for utility? These are just some of the contextual questions you need to answer before you can start designing your user experience.

Think about this: when you download an app, how much about the app do you know before you open it? If you heard about it from a friend, you probably at best have a one-sentence description of what the app is supposed to do. When you install and open it, you probably still have little idea of what to do with it. User experience is how the app takes you from being a somewhat random downloader and converts you to being a regular user of the app. If you think about the apps you use the most, you probably didn't read a user manual or asked for help to learn how to work it. You jumped in and quickly figured it out. Apps with great user experiences create the right visual and non-visual elements to orient people and build long-lasting relationships with them.

Creating the right user experience is a product of simplification, focus and iteration. You have no easier test of an app's user experience than by handing a phone with the app installed to a non-user and then watching them use it. Don't say anything and don't try to help, it's as if they were a random person who just installed the app from the app store. While you watch them, here are some things to help you think about the user experience of the app:

1. How does the user react to the app when it opens for the first time?
2. Where is the first touch the user makes after the app opens?
3. How much knowledge does the app expect of its users?
4. Does the app give proper visual cues to the user when it's busy performing an action?
5. Does it transition between screens smoothly?
6. Does the app lead the user through a task or does it wait for the user to find it?
7. Does the app feel slow, fast or both?

In app land, building a great user experience is very different than on a web site or PC application. Not only is there a tiny screen, but there is also no mouse, a small keyboard, limited battery, poor cellular connections, and individual circumstances, such as the user who might use an app while they are wedged between two people on the subway. To build a great user experience, you have to account for all of these factors. If you are building a communication app, then understand people are probably going to use your app when they are in a rush and need to get a message to someone else quick. If you are building a mapping app, then realize a lot of the times people will be standing on a corner, perhaps under an umbrella in a torrential downpour, looking down at your app to tell them where to go. Understanding the differences between these two contexts and how they apply to your app will allow you to make the right decisions when creating a user interface.

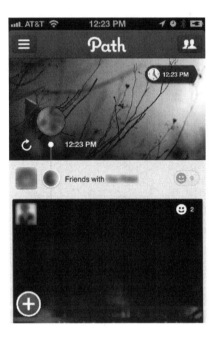

Figure 5: Path's iPhone app is critically acclaimed for its simple and elegant user experience

The human nature of user experience means that it is an intangible quantity. You can neither measure user experience nor perfectly specify what it is meant to be. It is simply the connection between a user and the app.

Reason #2: They Give Users a Reason to Come Back

A 2010 study completed by mobile app marketing and app analytics provider Localytics concluded that 26% of all apps downloaded by users are only opened once[8]. Mobile phone users are a notoriously fickle bunch, with the cost of doing something else being nothing more than a finger tap. This makes building an app something like competing on a reality television talent show. If users aren't engaged by your app, they will very quickly pull the rug from underneath and move on to something else. A great app takes the 5-10 seconds a first-time user might spend using the app and engages them enough to create a reason for them to open it again. If your app gives users no reason to come back, or even worse, gives them plenty of reason to never come back, you've failed at creating a good app.

Apps like Instagram, Facebook, and DrawSomething all created engaging experiences that brought the user back into their apps. For instance, Instagram and Facebook draw users back into their apps because they scratch an emotional need in their users. Be it narcissism or voyeurism, these social networking apps win users by making them feel good about themselves. For instance, when somebody posts something on your Facebook Timline, the Facebook mobile app notifies you by playing a sound and displaying a notification on your phone. Piqued by their own curiosity and excitement, users return to the app to read the comment.

Figure 6: The red notification flag draws users back into the
Facebook app

The emotional dependence created by social networks runs
deeper than push notifications sent to a mobile device. The
Facebook app is designed to constantly provide visual cues when a
user receives a new Facebook notification. The red marker
Facebook uses to denote a new notification stands out from the
blue background and is brightly visible from all points in the app.
Further, with a single glance down at the Facebook app, a user
knows their notification count. The user experience of the
Facebook app conveys this information very clearly and simply.
People come back to the app, open it up, see the flag and can either
go back to what they were doing or dig deeper into the app to see
the entire notification.

With apps like DrawSomething, users are similarly drawn back
into the app both by a need to seek entertainment and in response
to actions taken by other users. When an opponent in
DrawSomething finishes their round, the other player is again
notified right away of the event. The push notification they receive

allows them to open up the app and immediately view and react to whatever their opponent did. This creates a very easy end-user loop where users both seek out the app when they are looking entertainment and are called back into the app through push notifications delivered to the phone.

Reason #3: They are Designed to go Viral

Outside of revenue, the measuring stick for the success of any app is the number of users it has. If you are planning a free app and looking to recoup your investment via in-app advertising or even an acquisition, then you will need hundreds of thousands of users to be successful. DrawSomething had nearly 15 million users prior to being purchased by Zynga[9], and Instagram had almost 30 million users prior to its purchase by Facebook[10]. To hit these kinds of user numbers takes more than a flashy app description and a few dollars spent on Google Adwords. To achieve this type of growth, you need your app to go 'viral'.

As the name implies, going viral means achieving exponential user growth rates, most likely due to an infectious spread of your app through social media. In DrawSomething's case, its integration into Twitter and Facebook activity feeds allowed it to get visibility on the feeds of every user that joined. The postings on Facebook and Twitter of users completing games or inviting friends to join them were compelling enough that many people who saw them decided to download the app and give it a try. We'll go into more detail on specific features you can include in your app to increase its chances of going viral later on in the Marketing chapter.

3.3

What Makes a Bad App?

It's hard to figure out what the secret sauce is to creating a great app, but it's much easier to point out what makes a bad app. If a 'great' app is one that grows to either generate enough revenue to its creator or provide enough of a user base that can then be indirectly monetized, a bad app is one that fails to do either.

The list of bad apps is much longer than great ones, and includes some rather notable, high-profile failures. Perhaps the greatest flop in the app world to date has been Color, a location-based photo-sharing app that launched to great fanfare with $41 million in pre-launch funding in 2011. Other apps like Forecast, were great ideas, but for one reason or another failed to generate real user interest and were shuttered. More on that a little later.

In general, take heed the corpses of failed apps that litter the marketplace. The greatest lessons are often learned through failure. Here are a few things we can learn from failed apps to understand what makes a 'bad app':

Reason #1: They Are Buggy and/or Poorly Built

It should go without saying that a poorly built mobile application is a sure fire way to failure. Gone are the days of Windows XP when users tolerated, if not expected, applications to crash, screens to lock up and any of the myriad of bugs that litter the PC world. Traditional software companies such as Microsoft could live with releasing a buggy product because the update mechanisms built into Windows allowed them to deliver patches and fixes down the road to slowly stabilize the release over time. While all major mobile app marketplaces allow for the updating of apps through the app store, the mobile app user is much less likely to tolerate a crashing app. Mobile app users are a fickle, unforgiving bunch, especially when it comes to buggy apps. When faced with a crashing app, a mobile user will at best ignore the issue, but will more likely uninstall the app, and at worst write a negative review on the marketplace.

Thus, the traditional mantra of *release then patch* is a sure fire way to find your app listing flooded with negative reviews and your user base gone. Instead, in the mobile world, you need to focus on building high-quality releases that sacrifice functionality for great user experiences. One of our commandments of mobile app development is to release early and often, which means that your app releases will tend to be smaller in scope, with major changes happening over a period of releases rather than all in one shot.

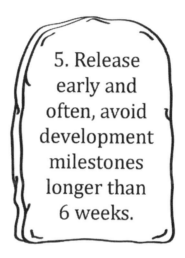

Figure 7: Focus on doing less in each release, the quality of your app will benefit

Creating a high-quality mobile app requires a relentless obsession with testing and bug fixing. As any professional software test engineer will tell you, this is a terribly difficult task. Creating high quality software requires more than just ad-hoc testing of your app. It requires a thought out plan in terms of scoping the functionality of your app to ease the test burden and ensure you deliver a high-quality app to your user base.

Reason #2: They do not scale

A GeekWire study conducted in 2011 identified *premature scaling* as the number 1 reason why high-tech startups fail[11]. While the GeekWire study focused on scaling business operations, part of the reason why companies are unable to scale successfully is that their technology is unable to scale with them. Scale in terms of mobile apps generally refers to the number of users using the app. However, scale isn't limited to just number of users, but rather any quantity of data that increases as the app gains more users. In the case of Instagram, scale meant an increased number of pictures being created, stored and saved via the service, which requires increased bandwidth and storage for the app to handle. Building a mobile app that responds and operates well with 10 users is no indication that it will work when there are 10,000, or 1 million users.

If you want your app to succeed, you should expect that eventually you will have millions of users on the app. When starting out this might seem like a far off dream that you choose to handle when it becomes an issue, but the truth about technology is that if your foundation isn't built from day one to handle large numbers of users, then it becomes increasingly difficult to change that as more layers are added on top of it. It's not necessary to test and verify that you app can handle 1 million users when you first ship it, but your developers need to design the architecture of the app with the clear vision that one day it will need to handle increased levels of scale without incurring massive engineering costs.

We cannot stress the importance of keeping scale in mind from the get go, as we have bear witness to massive software projects requiring complete re-writes because they were unable to handle increased scale. By far the most common reason we have seen software projects fail is that no architectural guidance was given to developers when they initially wrote the code for a product. Thus, by the time the application was scaled up to handle increased number of users, it keeled over and died because it couldn't handle the size. Don't let this be your app. Make sure your CTO or the lead developer of your app is well aware of your future growth goals and is designing the app's architecture to handle them.

Reason #3: They Have Poorly Thought Out User Experiences

As we've mentioned before, the best mobile apps have user experiences that are simple and make sense given the purpose of the app and the context of the user. On the flip side, apps that flop tend to be marked by confusing user interface elements and overly complex details that render them difficult to use.

A great example of poor user experience design is with the Color app. Color was released in 2011 to great fanfare. It was to enable location-based sharing of photos between strangers. While an excellent idea in concept, the design of the app totally failed to follow through on the promise of that idea.

One of the major faults of the Color app was that users would open it up and be presented with a completely empty screen, which was meant to fill up with pictures being shared by users nearby. The issue Color had was one common to all location based sharing apps: user density. The Color app was designed to show only photos being shared by other users of the Color app that were nearby, however, there wasn't enough user density in most major areas to fill even a small part of the screen. So when Color launched in the Summer of 2011, most users opened the app and were presented with an empty screen, as very few of them were actually in the vicinity of another Color users to see each other's photos. The initial reaction of most users was, "What now?" Color presented a blank screen, and no prompts or guide to get the user contributing to the app, which would in turn help reduce the user density issue. Most users closed the app after a minute or two of wondering what to do and never returned.

Color floundered from its release in 2011 and never met the expectations that its investors and management had predicted. In November of 2012, Color announced that it was shutting down.

Figure 8: Color's UI screens continually left users confused as to how they should use the app

Color's failure is emblematic of the problems faced with introducing location-based mobile apps. In retrospect, Color would have been well-served to either market the app in specific geographical areas such that every new user would sign up and actually be in the vicinity of other users or provide a walk-through first time experience which held the user's hand in creating and sharing a photo. Instead, users were left mostly to their own devices to figure out what to do with the app. Not surprisingly, what most people decided to do was close it and never open it again.

Reason #4: They Aren't Useful

At the end of the day, your app needs to have a purpose and be interesting to its audience. Unless you are building for utility, your app will need to entertain its users and create enough of a niche for itself that a user would return to use it. Underlying your app is a core idea or hypothesis you have come up with; if that idea is not engaging, then your app will fail. Further, with social networking app ideas, the usefulness of these apps is often correlated to the number of people using them. The idea could be great, but if it requires everybody in a user's circle of friends to use it in order to be useful, then your app is likely to fail.

In our commandments, we said that your app idea is less important than execution and that remains true. However, your app idea has to provide some value to its user. Otherwise, its existence is moot. There is no easy way to determine if your idea is good, but ask yourself some of these questions and think about your answers:

1. Why would someone use your app?
2. What do people use right now instead of this app?
3. Is there another app or service that users would expect to provide the functionality your app offers?
4. Is the problem you are looking to solve an *actual* problem people want to solve?
5. Is your app easy enough to use that a user would choose to use it rather than to live with the status quo?
6. Does your app require a certain number of users or friends to be using it to provide value?

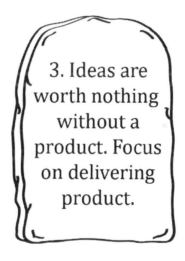

Figure 9: You need a product, not just a great idea

With these questions in mind, let's look at another failed app, Forecast. Forecast was an app designed to let users share their future destinations with their friends and gain visibility into where their friends would be in the future. The idea behind the app is at first glance very exciting: know where your friends are and where they're going to be. It operated as an aggregator atop Facebook and Foursquare and allowed users to create *Forecasts*, which were events in the future that they were planning to attend. Users could also see Forecasts created by their friends. Forecast didn't last long, and it was shut down in July 2012 after failing to gain any real user traction. Looking back, Forecast suffered from an idea that required too much effort on the part of the users and didn't achieve the necessary scale to make it a worthwhile product to use.

Figure 10: Forecast is an example of a 'great idea' that didn't translate into a 'great app'

People do want to know where their friends are and are going to be, but today, people can find that out through SMS, Facebook, or just by looking at an Outlook calendar. While none of those provide a perfect solution to solve the problem holistically, Forecast required users to input into the app the specifics of where and when the user will be in the future. As simple as their user interface was, the effort required to input this information was too great for most users to undertake, especially since the status quo mechanisms were simpler and required less effort. The motivation for a user to input this information was not strong enough to change their current behavior, and thus, the app languished with few users.

Compounding this is the reality that people wouldn't use the app unless their friends were using it, and the entire concept of Forecast was predicated on having entire social networks using the app. In retrospect, Forecast could have achieved greater success if it integrated already into people's online calendars and other scheduling tools, which already contained this information. By lowering the cost of using the app, Forecast could have increased the number of users on the app and started to deliver real value as more people used it.

3.4

Evaluating the Dani's List app

Dani's List is meant to help people answer the age-old question of "What is there to do today?" Whether it's an idle Sunday with your significant other or a few days in a foreign country, Dani's List is meant to provide a way for people to find, share and keep track of activities, sights, restaurants and past times that they'd like to try.

The idea behind Dani's List is by no means Earth-shatteringly unique. A cursory look at the App Store reveals a plethora of apps that provide some type of event discovery, restaurant guide, or personal to-do list management. However, that other people have entered this space is not reason enough for us to abandon the idea. Remember, the market for apps is huge and you shouldn't be put off because someone has already implemented your idea. In fact, given that the Apple App Store alone has over 800,000 apps, you should expect that, for most ideas, there will already be 1 or 2 apps that do similar sounding things. Another thing to remember is that the app space is very nascent. It's very difficult for any single app to have a complete monopoly position in its market. In particular, the location-based discovery space that Dani's List will compete in has no established leader, and no app has achieved brand name recognition like a Foursquare or a Shazam.

Developing Customer Scenarios

We started with a basic idea of what we saw as the purpose of Dani's List. The next step was to flesh out this idea and create a set of user scenarios that depict the exact situations we see people in while using the app. Ideas are very general statements and they tend to hide a lot of the nuances of the problems. An idea is not enough to build an app. You need to know exactly in which situations you envision your app will be used and which ones it won't. More importantly, you need to write these down so that at any point in the development of the app you can use these scenarios as a guide for making good design decisions and prioritizing bug fixes. Scenarios are designed to keep your customer's needs and perspective in mind and to allow you to frame the decisions you make based on what might serve them best.

With Dani's List, let's enumerate a few key scenarios that we think describe what people might use the app for:

- "Buon giorno! I've just landed in Venice. I'm here for a couple of days and need some places to go or *ristoranti* to try while I am here."
- "Good morning Seattle! What a beautiful Sunday. It looks like the sun has decided to make a rare appearance today. I want to go outside and bask in its glory. What are some things I can do in the sun?"
- "I don't know honey, what do you want to do tonight?"
- "You know, one day I want to show you the Columbia University campus and where I used to live in undergrad. I'm putting it on our list!"
- "Wow, watching the Hare Krishnas chant in Union Square was actually quite soothing. I think people would like it. I'm adding that to Dani's List."

As odd as they sound, these scenarios illustrate exactly the types of situations people might look to use Dani's List. Scenarios aren't meant to be functional descriptions of your app (that comes later). Instead, they specify the types of situations and problems in which people should be able to look to your app in order to solve. We'll refer back to these scenarios as we progress through the development of Dani's List and use them to drive our decisions around the design and functionality of the app. Later on in the book, we will go over how to create *Scenario Documents* that you can use to plan and drive your development process.

Can Dani's List be a Great App?

Now that we have a better idea of what scenarios we see people using Dani's List for, we need to step back and ask ourselves: Can we make Dani's List be a great app? Now we are not psychic and probably neither are you, so this is more of an existential question more than one with a concrete answer. As we mentioned earlier in the book, a great app is as much a product of luck as it is of great design and engineering. Nevertheless, earlier on in the chapter, we outlined a few traits that separate great apps from merely good ones:

- Reason #1: Great apps deliver great user experiences

- Reason #2: Great apps give users a reason to come back

- Reason #3: Great apps are designed to go viral

With these 3 principles in mind, let's see how we can go about designing Dani's List so that we best position it to succeed:

Great apps deliver great user experiences

This is a nebulous trait, as there isn't one standard definition of what a 'great user experience' is. However, the key to designing a great user experience is to understand in depth how people will use Dani's List and the situations they might be in when they do. Once we have a better idea of these user contexts, we can then create a user experience that is tailored for the environment and tasks people would want to complete while in these contexts.

The scenarios we fleshed out in the previous section give us some sense of this, but let's now go a step further and derive some general statements about how people will look to use Dani's List:

1. People will look to the app for inspiration or to generate ideas of things they can possibly occupy their time with over the period of a few days.
2. Generally, people will use the app for browsing and planning while they are stationary and probably while bantering back and forth with one or more other people.
3. People will need a simple way of selecting activities they

find in the app that they are interested in doing and placing them on their own personal to-do list in the app.

4. Users will typically have a few (probably less than 3) constraints they will want to use when finding new things to do. These constraints can include: Distance from their current location; Type of activity (something to eat vs. something to do); Amount they want to spend; Current time of day; Current weather; Desire to be outdoors or indoors.

5. People will come back to their own personal list of activities periodically throughout the day. In these cases, they'll likely be crossing things off that they've done, looking for the next thing to do, or digging in to get more details (like the address, contact information, photo) of the next activity they are heading towards. In these situations, people can expect to be moving about and not completely stationary.

6. Some people, upon completing an activity they liked, will want to share that experience with their friends who might also one day be in the area. Most likely they'll want to share this via Facebook or Twitter.

This list is by no means exhaustive, but these statements give us a better sense of the environment someone might be in when they use the app along with the type of actions that would be most important in them. When we get to designing the app, we'll use these statements to guide how we layout the user interface (UI) and what functionalities we will include. Later on, we will also use these statements to create a *Functional Specification Document* that will serve as blue print for the development of Dani's List.

Great apps give users a reason to come back

We mentioned this earlier in the chapter, but it's worth mentioning twice: only 26% of all apps downloaded are ever used twice. That's a frighteningly bad statistic for an Appster and one we need to tackle very early in our design process. There's no benefit to acquiring users who only download an app once, so when creating Dani's List we need to be sure that there is enough of a hook in the app that people have a reason to return to use it.

With Dani's List, there are a few things we can do during the first launch of the app and other subsequent events to ensure users come back to use the app again:

- When a user launches the app for the first time, instead of showing an empty list of things to do on their personal list, the app should open into a screen that immediately lists activities that other people have entered into the app and which are geographically close to the user.
- During the first launch, we can encourage the user to sign up for an account on Dani's List. The benefit of this is we can then create a conversation with them outside of the app through email. Email is an excellent mechanism to remind users about the app by sending them a periodic notification that could include activities near their last location that might be interesting to them. Ideally, an email sent by the app to the user would encourage the user to open the app up again and try it.
- Facebook integration of the app can encourage users to come back to the app when they see activities created/completed by their friends pop up on their news feed.
- Facebook integration can also allow user to click 'add activity to my list' on activities created by friends. Upon clicking, what this could do is open the app (or if on a desktop, open a web browser) and the item is immediately added to the user's personal list of activities.
- An email can be sent to the user whenever a Facebook friend has also signed up for the app.
- Push notifications are another way of reminding users to use the app. For instance, when a new activity near them appears, a push notification is sent to their phone, encouraging them to revisit the app. We need to be cautious with push notifications, however, as there is a very fine line between providing useful information to the user and spamming them.

These are just a few brainstorms on how we can improve user retention within the app. We'll use these ideas later on in the book when we set about designing the actual Dani's List app.

Have your own idea for an app? Flesh it out by completing the first three sections of the *Idea to Appster Worksheet* on the next page. This exercise will help you think through your idea and develop it to include some of the characteristics we talked about in this chapter. A downloadable copy of the full worksheet, illustrated with examples from Dani's List, is available on the *Idea to Appster* website. Visit www.ideatoappster.com/book now to get your free copy.

1. App Idea: *The purpose of this app, in 20 words or less.*

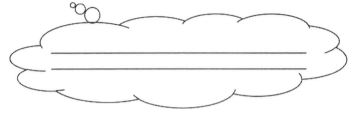

2. User Scenarios: *Quote what people might say in situations they would use this app.*

Figure 11: Idea to Appster Worksheet - Brainstorming the Idea. Steps 1 and 2, the App Idea and User Scenarios.

3. Good to Great: *Great apps deliver a great user experience, a reason to come back, and an opportunity to go viral.*

A great user experience:
Derive some general statements about how people will look to use this app.

- _____
- _____
- _____
- _____

A reason to come back:
List a few "hooks" that can be used in the app to ensure users come back again.

- _____
- _____
- _____
- _____

An opportunity to go viral:
Identify seeds for users of the app that could sprout a viral spread to non-users.

- _____
- _____
- _____
- _____

Figure 12: Idea to Appster Worksheet - Brainstorming the Idea.
Step 3 – Going from Good to Great.

4.

App Economics 101

Let's face it, you probably aren't entering the mobile app space purely out of a curiosity for new technology. You want to make money! The economics of creating an app depend on a variety of factors, such as the type of app you are making, how you source development, and your strategy for monetization. At the end of the day, there are only a few ways to monetize an app, which can be boiled down to some variation of paid downloads, advertising, and in-app purchases. Which one of these you choose will depend on your app, its customer base and its competitive landscape, along with your expectations for return on investment.

Even if you have no plans to directly monetize your app, there exists an additional opportunity for you to generate money through your app: acquisition. The bubbling hype that surrounds mobile apps along with the appetite for established companies to bolster their app and talent portfolios introduces the possibility of being acquired as another form of monetization. The purchase of Instagram by Facebook in 2012 for roughly $1 billion is a prime example of this type of sale. Instagram, up to that point, had a grand total of $0 in revenue and no short-term plans for monetization. However, Instagram's explosive popularity saw it grow to ~30 million users in 18 months[12]. In the case of Instagram, it was the possibility of monetizing a dedicated user base of 30 million people that made the company so valuable to Facebook and other social media sites. The lesson to learn from Instagram, and other high profile acquisition targets, like DrawSomething, is that in the absence of a monetization plan for your app, your focus must to be to get your app onto as many people's phones as possible.

Realistically, you shouldn't enter app development with acquisition as your only monetization strategy. While it is certainly a possibility that an external firm might want to acquire your app and your team in the future, you will be hard pressed to find investors willing to finance your app without some thought given to more traditional sources of monetization.

Monetization covers only the revenue side of app development; you also need to consider the expenses involved in running an app and the investment you'll need to get it off the ground. Just creating an app from scratch and getting it deployed to the app store requires a large investment of time and money. Once your app has gone live, you will need to factor in maintenance, hosting and marketing costs to keep your app growing. Given the large upfront costs of app development, it's likely that your app will take time to reach profitability. Thus, you will need to take this into account when you think about how best to finance your app.

In this chapter we will break down the revenue side of the mobile app space and go into further depth on the monetization strategies and choosing the best one. After that, we will provide some insight on the expense side of the equation, along with a discussion just how much it will cost to get your app built. By the end of this chapter, you should have good idea of the economics of mobile apps and how they apply to your app idea.

4.1

Monetization

Monetization is just a fancy word for how you will generate revenue with your app. Revenue is an accounting term used to describe money generated through sales. In the world of traditional PC/Mac software, monetization is achieved normally through product licensing where the customer either pays a single price for the product or a per-unit price depending on some other factor, such as the number of people who will use the software. It's not unusual for desktop software like Microsoft Office to retail for hundreds of dollars. As we mentioned earlier in the book, the introduction of apps upended this model of high up-front pricing for software. When it comes to mobile apps, they are sold normally on a per-user basis, starting at $0.99. However, many apps are sold free of charge and rely on either in-app purchases or advertising to generate revenue. In general, there are 3 basic models of app-monetization to choose from: up-front pricing, in-app purchases, and advertising. Let's take a look at each of these models:

Up-front pricing

As the name implies, this model relies on charging some amount of money for the user to download your app from a marketplace like the Apple App Store and Google Play. Typically, the price developers charge for an app ranges from $0.99 up to $1,000.00 and beyond. Choosing the right price point for your app depends on many different factors: the type of app you're building, your competition, and your target customer base. In general, utility apps are the easiest to sell to customers since they provide tangible value to them. On the other hand, social networking apps are a poor choice for paid downloads since they depend on a large number of people using the app to gain traction and achieve success.

If you decide to charge money up-front for people to download your app, there's a very simple equation to predict how much revenue your app will generate:

$$Revenue = Price \times Quantity$$

The lower the price you charge, the more copies of the app you will need to sell in order to achieve a certain revenue target. On the other hand, the higher you set your app price, the fewer copies you will need to sell to achieve the same goal. In general, mobile app economics mirror those of normal goods you would buy in a store. The higher the price you charge, the lower quantity of goods you can expect to sell.

Determining what the optimal price point is in order to maximize revenue is a difficult exercise and often requires trial-and-error analysis of sale changes at different price points. A good strategy for finding the price point that maximizes your revenue is to start selling your app at a higher price point and slowly work your way down with incremental price cuts. Using the analysis tools provided by the marketplace your app is on, you can analyze how many more downloads you were able to drive for each price reduction. You could approach it the other way around with incremental price increases, but customers generally tend to look negatively towards price increases! Luckily, the App Store and Google Play marketplaces make it easy for you to set different prices for your apps and change them as you see fit.

If you want to take a more mathematically rigorous approach to coming up with a price for your app, there are a couple of pricing models you can use to help find it: value-based and cost-based pricing.

Value-based pricing

With value-based pricing you set the price of your app based on the dollar value that a customer would gain by using it. For example, if you have an app that allows people to find the cheapest gas station near them, you can a build a value-based pricing model to quantify the savings that an average user would receive by using this app over a year and then derive the appropriate selling price of your app.

If your cheap gas finding app does work, you can then put together a simple model to understand the savings that might be delivered to the customer:

Let's define the following variables:

- Average $ per gallon saved by using your app (G)
- Average # of miles driven per year by a user (M)
- Average fuel economy (miles / gallon) for a user (MPG)

Thus, the average annual value delivered to customer (V_c):
$$V_c = G \times (M/MPG)$$

This is a start, but our model is still a bit basic. Not every customer is going to use the app to extract the same amount of savings (G). One way to make our model more accurate is to model three different customer types: low, medium, and high, which reflect the different levels of gas savings achieved by using our app. 'Low' reflects customers that only achieve marginal savings through the use of the app. 'Medium' reflects customers achieving an average amount of savings. 'Large' would be customers who achieve the greatest amount of savings through our the app. If we model out these three customer types, we can then average the savings per user to get a more confident view at the savings achieved through the use of your app.

	Scenario 1	Scenario 2	Scenario 3
G	$0.02	$0.10	$0.15
M	20,000 miles	20,000 miles	20,000 miles
MPG	20 mpg	20 mpg	20 mpg
V_c	$20	$100	$150

Figure 13: Comparison of savings between Low, Medium and High Scenarios

Average Annualized Savings:
($20 + $100 + $150) / 3 = $90

With our revised model we've computed that the average savings over the course of a year through the use of our app is an estimated $90. Now that we have this number, we can set the price of the app to be some portion of the $90 in savings a customer can expect to achieve with the app. Economics teaches us that a rational consumer that expects to save V_c by using our app would purchase it at a price P, where $P \leq V_c$. Given that a customer can expect to save $90 per year with our app, then we should set the price somewhere between $0 and $90.

The downside to the value-based pricing approach is that it relies on many assumptions on our part on the behavior of the customer. While this poses some difficulty, we can overcome it by performing market research on our customer prior to development in hopes of understanding their driving habits. By using surveys, interviews or government transportation data, we can reduce the variability in our calculations by coming up with better estimates for our model inputs. Another drawback of value-based pricing model is that it does not take into account any notion of competition and basis itself solely on the merits of the app. If there were already other apps that help users save gas, we'd need to take into account those price points when coming up with the final price of the app.

The value-based pricing approach works very well with utility apps, as these apps actually deliver measurable value to their users. Games and informational apps aren't easily analyzed using this mechanism, as the value the customer derives is something much more intangible.

Cost-based pricing

Cost-based pricing takes on the pricing problem from the developer's perspective. With cost-based pricing you are setting the price of your product based on the average per-unit cost of producing it plus some markup that you'd like to earn as profit.

Let's define the following variables:

- Average Cost per download (AC)
- Markup per download (M)

Price per download (P):
$$P = AC + M$$

The equation for determining the Average Cost (AC) per download of your app is:

- Average Variable Cost per download (AVC)
- Average Fixed Cost per download (AFC)

Average Cost (AC):
$$AC = AVC + AFC$$

With mobile app development, the Average Variable Cost of producing a new download of the app is almost always 0 (AVC = 0), since selling an additional copy doesn't require any further cost on your end. On the other hand, app development has large fixed costs that are paid independent of the number of copies of the app sold, such as development, marketing, and hosting. To estimate the Average Fixed Cost per unit, you will need to assume a certain number of app downloads (Q) and then allocate the total fixed costs (TFC) to each unit based on that quantity. Our equation above then becomes:

Let's define the following variables:

- Number of app downloads or Quantity (Q)
- Average Fixed Cost per download (AFC)

Total Fixed Costs (TFC):
$$TFC = AFC \times Q$$

Now lets revisit our equation for Price per download (P) above and replace some variables to find a new equation for price based on cost:

We know Price per download (P):
$$P = AC + M$$

Since we know AC = AVC + AFC and we assume Average Variable Cost (AVC) for an app is $0, then:
$$AC = \$0 + AFC$$
$$AC = AFC$$

Therefore we can replace AC with AFC:
$$P = AFC + M$$

Now, if we rearrange the equation for Total Fixed Cost (TFC) from above as follows:
$$TFC = AFC \times Q$$
$$AFC = TFC / Q$$

We can now replace Average Fixed Cost (AFC) in our equation for Price per download (P):
$$P = TFC / Q + M$$

Thus if the Total Fixed Cost for developing your app is $100,000, and you'd expect to sell 20,000 copies, and want to earn $0.50 per download:

Price per download (P):
$$P = \$100,000/20,000 + \$0.50$$
$$P = 5 + 0.50$$
$$P = \$5.50$$

Thus, using the cost-based pricing model, it suggests that we price our app at $5.50 per download.

The downside with cost-based pricing is that it makes a big assumption on the desired quantity of downloads. If we are unable to achieve the 20,000 downloads we assumed in the model, then we may potentially end up losing money as our per unit cost will go up. Further, another drawback of cost-based pricing is that it may potentially cause us to charge lower than what a customer would be willing to pay for the app. If the app delivered tremendous value for its users, it's conceivable that they would be willing to pay $10 or $20 per download, but the cost-based pricing model does not take that into account.

In the end, there is no magic bullet for coming up with the price of your app as each model offers both advantages and disadvantages. These models are good for estimating the future financial performance of an app prior to development, as they at least give you some basis to create a revenue model from. However, once your app is ready for sale, you can use these models to figure out a starting price point to sell your app. From here, use incremental price decreases and analyze the affect they have on downloads of your app. With a little trial-and-error, you should be able to identify the price point that maximizes your revenue.

Promotions

Never underestimate the importance psychology plays in a consumer's buying decision. Promotions, giveaways, and sales are tried-and-true mechanisms to increase revenue by giving customers the sense that they are getting a limited time deal. In the mobile app space, promotions have become an effective tool to attract audiences and gain additional sales. Instead of charging a flat price of $5 per download, you could set the price of your app to be $7, and then drive sales by offering a ~30% off promotion to new customers. At the end of the day, the economics are the same for you, but your customers will believe they have snagged quite the deal!

Furthermore, by using promotions to drive sales you open up new channels to advertise and gain users. For example, there are numerous web sites designed to aggregate mobile app promotions and bring them to customers that might be interested. One great example of such a web site is *Free App a Day* (http://www.freeappaday.com), which offers free apps to its customer base for a limited time. Other online communities, like *Reddit*, have their own dedicated sub-groups for users to spread promotions for apps. One of the largest of the Reddit subgroups is named *AppHookup* and has almost 10,000 subscribers.

Since there is no direct cost to you for giving away a free version of your app, promotional web sites and online communities are a great way to generate downloads and revenue for your app.

'Freemium'

The concept behind the *freemium* monetization model is to let users download the app for free, and then provide premium functionality or other value-adds that a user can choose to buy after using the free version of the app. Freemium typically manifests itself in three ways: trial mode/paid upgrade, in-app purchases, and pay-walls.

Trial mode / Paid upgrade

Much like the *shareware* model of desktop software, this model offers one version of the app for free and a paid-version of the app as an upgrade. The paid version of the app usually contains additional functionality or levels for the user to complete. If you remember the game Doom from the early 1990s, this is a classic example of a shareware app. Note that with this model you will need to release and support two separate versions of your app: a free and paid version.

In-app purchases

A more modern twist to the Trial mode/Paid upgrade model is the concept of in-app purchases. With this model, users are able to purchase virtual goods within the app for real money, which can range from buying upgrades, sending gifts or obtaining additional game opportunities. Whereas the Trial mode/Paid upgrade model switches the entire version of the app based on an upgrade, the in-app purchase model enables users to use the same version of the app and purchase virtual goods within it.

'Pay-walls'

With informational apps like a newspaper or magazine reader, a recent trend for monetization has been to introduce a *pay-wall*, which separates free content from premium content that requires purchase to view.

A great example of a pay-wall in action is the New York Times app. If you download the app and open it up, all of the articles listed in the front page of the app are free to view. However, if a user wants to read any articles that are beyond the front-page, they are prompted to subscribe to the New York Times before being able to view the articles. Another twist on the pay-wall model is to introduce a maximum number of articles a reader can read for free per month, after which they'd be required to purchase a subscription to view more. With the New York Times web site, you are able to view 20 articles per month free. After the 20th viewing of an article, a user is required to subscribe to the New York Time to view any more articles.

The freemium model is very compelling to an app developer, as the free-download component gets the app onto people's phones and then premium functionality is offered at a later time to the user. Recently the freemium model has gained rapid popularity to become the defacto monetization model for mobile apps. In 2011, it is estimated that roughly 39% of total app revenue was generated through a freemium model. By 2015, this is projected to increase to 64% of total app revenue[13].

The concept of freemium was first pioneered in gaming apps, where users were offered the ability to purchase weapons upgrades and send virtual gifts from within the app. From here, the concept has spread across the mobile app space and can be found in all app categories, from social networking to informational apps. Zynga, the company behind Farmville, and Cityville, is a freemium pioneer in the mobile space. For companies like Zynga that produce social-games, the freemium model allows them to build up a huge number of users with the free app download while offering clear paths within the app for the user to purchase additional functionality.

Both the Apple App Store and Google Play provide a platform that app developers can use to wire their app logic for in-app purchases directly into the credit card processing provided by each marketplace.

The psychology behind the freemium model is hard to beat. By foregoing any purchase price at the time of download, users are incentivized to download the app and try it out. Good freemium functionality provides a limited free experience that allows the user to perform a subset of the app's functionality, then offers functionality that is a natural extension of the freely offered functions as a freemium purchase. Freemium apps are designed to tap into the psychology of the user by creating strong incentives for users of the app to ante up and pay for additional functionality. Once users have downloaded and begun to use the app, the chances of them paying for additional functionality go up significantly.

An excellent example of freemium functionality is the Remember-the-Milk to-do list app. In the free download, a user is able to create any number of tasks they wish, but they are limited to one sync every 24 hours of their app data to the web. To view their to-do list on a laptop using a normal web browser, a user needs the Remember-the-Milk app to sync any tasks they may have added through their phone to the web. If the user is only allowed one sync per day, then the app becomes significantly less useful as a user is unable to manage their tasks from both their phone and laptop. The freemium functionality in Remember-the-milk is effective because it allows the user to build-up a dependence on the app through its free to-do list functionality. However, as a user increases their use of the app, the limitation of 1 sync per day becomes very constraining. At that point, the user has conceivably invested time and effort to enter their tasks into the app, so the cost of switching away from Remember-the-milk to a completely free app are very high, thus making the user more likely to pay the $5/month.

Designing good freemium functionality means understanding how users will use your app and identifying the most important concepts to a user. Here are some examples of freemium functionality that popular apps have offered:

Name	Category	Freemium Functionality
New York Times	Informational	Users can read only front-page articles, require upgrade to subscription to view other sections.
Remember-the-Milk	Utility	Users limited to 1 sync of tasks to cloud per day for free. Unlimited syncs offered for $5 / month.
Farmville	Gaming	Users earn "farm coins" which can be used to buy crops and animals via an in-app marketplace.
Chess-with-Friends	Gaming	Free version of app is ad-supported, with users forced to view ads after each move. Upgrading to paid version eliminates all ads within the app

Figure 14: Examples of 'freemium' functionality

Display Advertising

For free apps, the most common approach to earning revenue is through display advertising. If you've browsed the Internet over the past 15 years or so, you'll recognize display ads as the banner advertisements that usually appear at the top and/or sides of popular web sites.

As an Appster, you don't need to create these ads yourself, or in any which way solicit people to advertise on your site. Instead, you'll generally work through third-party brokers, called ad networks, that provide both the advertising and technical components you'll need to display them within your app. Ad networks serve as aggregators of advertising inventory, who then turn around and sell that inventory to agencies looking to initiate marketing campaigns against targeted demographics of users. Since you are a building an app, you are creating inventory that advertising networks will purchase from you and that's how you generate revenue.

Display advertisements come in many different varieties, and the model you adopt will depend on which ad network you work with. In general, mobile display advertising works the same as traditional web advertising with three generally accepted revenue models: CPM, CPC, and CPA

- **CPM (cost per thousand impressions)**
With the CPM model, you earn revenue based on the number of impressions delivered to your app's user base. An impression is merely the display of an ad to a user and does not require any click or action to be done by the user. The average CPM you can expect to receive in mobile can range from $0.20 to $5.00 CPM.

- **CPC (cost per click)**
As the name implies, you earn revenue based on the user clicking on an advertisement in your app.

- **CPA (cost per action)**
With CPA, the advertiser pays you based on your user completing some action. (i.e. signing up for a service, a form being filled, etc.)

The model you choose to adopt with your app depends on which advertising network you work with to display ads in your app. There are a plethora of mobile ad networks you can work with, with a few notable examples being *AdMob* (owned by Google), *iAd* and *inMobi*.

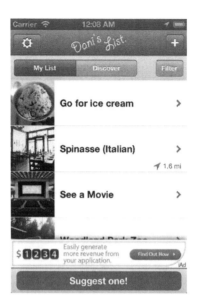

Figure 15: An iAd powered display ad embedded within Dani's List appears near the bottom of the screen

Figure 16: Overlay display ads (aka 'interstitial ads') which display on top of app content are very common in Zynga apps

Display advertising only starts to yield significant revenue when your app achieves a high degree of usage. Thus, you shouldn't rely on advertising revenue to be a large revenue generator in the early stages of your app. It's likely that you'll earn fractions of a cent on a CPC basis, which even in the most optimistic of click through rates (the percentage of people who actually click on the ads) would yield a few dollars per [TK]. However, as your app grows in adoption, you can expect your advertising revenue to increase along with it. According to AdWhirl, mobile iPhone apps that are amongst the top 100 free apps earn anywhere from $400 - $5000 a day from advertising alone!

Generally, the amount you earn on a CPC or CPM basis within your app is going to depend on the audience you are able to provide to the ad network you work with. In general, marketers are much more willing to pay higher rates to advertise on an app that has a well-known, quantifiable audience. The more readily a marketer is able to identify the group of users on your app, the higher the quality of advertising they can deliver. For instance, if you collect age, gender and location information within your app and feed them into an ad network, you should expect to see the CPC and CPM rates you earn go up substantially. Furthermore, if you market your app such that it is targeted towards a specific demographic, that too will help increase your advertising revenue.

Integrating mobile display advertising into your app is relatively straightforward. Most ad networks have developed components for all major mobile platforms that your developer simply needs to wire into the UI of your app. You can then customize the types of ads displayed and track analytics of your ad performance by using a web portal provided by the ad network.

When considering display ads, one important decision you will need to make is in the placement and size of the ads. The most popular way of displaying ads in a mobile app is with a banner that sits either below or atop the display area of your app. The disadvantage to this is that the advertisements can take away from the aesthetic of your app, in addition to constraining the available area you have for your UI. Another way of integrating display ads is to display ads in a full screen overlay in your app. This type of full screen ad is call an *interstitial* ad. For instance, if you've played a Zynga mobile game, after the completion of a turn or action, you will be displayed an almost full-page advertisement overtop of the app. After a period of time, you can click 'continue' which dismisses the advertisement and returns you to the app. The advantage of moving to a full screen approach to display ads is that you are likely to receive higher rates for that space and you are not cluttering the user interface of your app by shoehorning an advertising banner into it. The downside is that you are sticking large advertisements into the faces of your customers.

Content Advertising

Instead of display ads, another approach to monetization is through the creation of opportunities for sponsorship of content within your app. Twitter or Facebook each have the concept of *Sponsored Stories*, where news feed items and tweets are sponsored by a brand or other advertisers. These sponsored stories resemble content that might have been generated by a user using the app, but they're actually advertisements. For example, if you are building a photo-sharing app, you could enable advertisers to sponsor certain photos that anyone in the app can see.

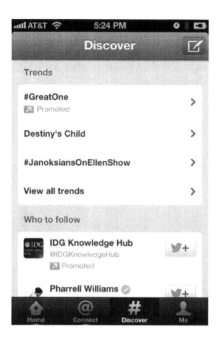

Figure 17: Twitter allows advertisers to sponsor hashtags (i.e.
#GreatOne) and profiles within their app

However, as content advertising is more ingrained into your
app and revolves around your app's user concepts, you will not be
able to work with most display networks. Traditional display
advertising relies on the standardization of ad inventory, which is
achieved through the integration of your app with a component
provided by the network. In a content-based scheme, the
advertising inventory you are creating is specific to your app and
hence you will need to develop your own capabilities to work with
agencies and advertisers to integrate them into your app. This will
likely require additional technical work to create the management
facilities necessary for advertisers to purchase and manage their
inventory within your app.

If you are able to create effective inventory for advertisers to
sponsor content in your app, it is likely that you will earn
considerably higher CPM/CPCs than you'd normally earn with
traditional display advertising. However, you will require substantial
investment and need to achieve an equally substantial scale of users

before you will realistically be able to open your app up to this monetization scheme.

4.2

Investment

Building an app is not cheap. That's the bad news. The good news is that once you get an app built, it doesn't cost much to keep it up and running. Mobile app development is largely a fixed cost endeavor, one that requires a lump sum investment up front to get the app designed and developed. Once your app has reached the marketplace, the cost for you to sell each additional copy of it, the marginal cost, is relatively low. In fact, the major per-unit cost you will incur selling an additional copy of the app through the marketplace is the commission you will pay to either Apple or Google for the sale. Even when it comes to marketing your app, there is no rule stating you have to spend any money at all to market it. The beauty of social media is that you can create viral buzz around your product with absolutely no paid advertising. It's not easy, but a social-media focused marketing campaign has proven a path to success for Instagram and DrawSomething, both of which spent little to no money on active advertising.

When developing an app, the costs you will incur largely will fall into these buckets: prototyping, design, engineering, hosting and commissions.

Prototyping

The first step of developing an app usually involves mocking up the UI and coming up with a visual look for the app using a prototyping toolkit. A mobile app prototype is usually a series of non-functional mockups of the UI designed to illustrate the basic concepts and user experience principles of your app. The toolkits to produce mobile app mockups range from the cheap and basic (using standard tools like PowerPoint), to complete prototyping suites, like Balsamiq and Photoshop, that can cost hundreds of dollars.

The important thing to remember about prototyping is that you are conveying a sketch of your ideas. You'll use this prototype to give investors, developers, designers and future customers an idea of what it is you are trying to build. A well-designed prototype will save you time and money down the road when it comes to engineering, as your developers will have a better idea from the start about what they will be building.

Nevertheless, there is little benefit in spending inordinate amounts of time and money creating highly realistic and immersive prototypes - they are just prototypes! Remember our second commandment: your idea will change. Expect that your prototype will have a very short life expectancy.

Figure 18: Don't spend too much time prototyping, your app will likely change once you start developing it

Here are a few different tools for app prototyping along with how much they cost:

Tool	Description	Price
PowerPoint / Keynote	Copy and paste your way to a prototype using prebuilt PowerPoint and Keynote templates.	$50 - $100
Balsamiq	Create clickable mockups using a stand-alone designer produced by Balsamiq software.	$80
Photoshop	Adobe's flagship design software allows you to create realistic mockups with full-color rendering and highly detailed screen designs.	$200+

Figure 19: Comparison of prototyping tools for apps

Design

After creating a prototype, your next major investment will be to work with a Graphic Designer to create the visual elements that will come to form the look and feel of your app. This includes items like the app icons, logo, buttons, fonts and color scheme choices. Depending on the amount of customization you are specifying beyond what is provided to you by your mobile platform, the amount of time and money spent on a designer will vary.

Typically, a designer will use tools such as Adobe's Photoshop to take the visual elements you have mocked up in your prototype to create a series of image files at different resolutions designed to fit the different types of mobile devices that your app will run (i.e. if it's an Android device, you might want to support both the smaller Galaxy Nexus phone along with the 7-inch tablet Nexus 7, each requiring their own graphics properly sized for their screen dimensions). In general, the more devices you are looking to support, the more time and effort will need to go into the design phase to make sure everything looks right from device to device. Additionally, supporting portrait and landscape displays for your app requires additional design work, as two different sets of resources will need to be created. Your need for a professional designer depends on your comfort level with creating the look and feel of your app, along with your ability to use tools like Photoshop to generate the necessary image resources that can be used by your engineers. Do not underestimate the value that a great designer can bring your app, as they will be able to guide you in creating the right visual experience to engage your users and improve retention.

Fortunately, finding good designers to help you on your project is much easier than finding engineers (more on that later). There are two major avenues you can use to find a designer for your app: you can bid-out your project on an auction basis through marketplaces, such as *99designs.com*, or you can seek out freelance designers to help you out on a contractual basis.

Design Marketplaces

When you use web sites like *99designs.com*, you are essentially auctioning off the work you need done to a pool of designers. Each of whom can choose to take a stab at your requirements and create a design. At the end of the auction, you pick the design submitted that you like the best, and the person who created gets paid a flat-rate that you specify at the time you created the auction.

Using a design marketplace like 99designs.com is fairly straight-forward:

- Specify the work you need done (i.e. "I need a logo designed" or "I need art work created for my mobile app") and how much you are willing to pay.
- Outline any conditions or parameters around the work you are bidding out. These conditions or parameters let you specify such things as the colors you want the designer to work with or the image resolutions you need.
- Submit your job (called 'contests') to the marketplace. Once your contest goes live, designers from all over the world can submit their drawings and design concepts based off your requirements.

- Over the course of the lifetime of your contest, usually a week, you can provide feedback to and work with designers who have submitted concepts to have it refined and improved to fit your needs.
- Once your contest closes, you select the best submission and the designer who created it is paid the amount you had originally specified. After the close of the contest, all the rights to the intellectual property created by the designer become yours.

Design marketplaces are a simple, effective way to farm out small design tasks that might not require a full-time designer to work on. If you are just looking for a logo or a set of small icons and buttons, then we highly recommend this approach as you are very likely to get very good results for a small investment of money.

Working with Freelance Graphic Designers

Some projects are too big for a design marketplace and you'd be better served seeking out a freelance designer to work on your app. A freelancer will usually bill an hourly rate while they create the visual design of your app and produce the necessary resources to support it. If you are building a gaming or informational app, you should strongly consider working with a single freelance graphic designer on your project. These types of apps usually require significant design work, both to decide on the final look and feel and to produce the plethora of image files, logos, and other design outputs to support the app.

You can find freelance graphic designers on *Craigslist* or through your own *LinkedIn* network. Web sites such as *Elance.com*, and *Freelancer.com* are online freelance boards where freelance designers offer their services to interested parties. Further, *Elance* profiles include community feedback, such as ratings from other clients who have used a particular vendor along with centralized billing facilities, which make it easy to staff up and down your company with freelance help.

When looking for freelance designers it's important to focus on their portfolio of past work to judge their suitability for your project. If the designer doesn't have any portfolio items showing the work they have done on mobile projects, be wary. When looking at a designer's profile, you should be looking for the right alignment between style elements that you like and elements that the designer has used in their past work (e.g., if you are looking for a clean, uncluttered look, has the designer's past work shown that they can create that type of experience?).

The rates that freelance designers charge to work on your project will depend on the depth of their portfolio, along with the effort they judge to be required to complete your work. In general, for a mobile app, you should look to pay $50 - $75 per hour for an experienced, US-based graphic designer. Typically, over the course of an app like Dani's List that has only a few visual elements to design, you can expect to spend less than $1,000 to have all of the necessary resources produced.

Engineering

This shouldn't come as a surprise, but your greatest investment in time, money and effort on your app quest is engineering, or put more simply: getting it built. *Engineering* is the process of taking your prototype, along with the designs, and having a team of programmers build, test and submit your app to the relevant marketplace. If we were building a house, engineering is the part where the house actually gets built. Unlike building a house, you simply can't grab a person off the curb of a Home Depot and have them build your app. The programmers that can write apps for the iOS and Android platforms are in very high demand and thus are very expensive to hire. Programming is a highly skilled profession which requires years of training and experience for one to be simply proficient. This specialized knowledge makes hiring engineers a very expensive endeavor, as experienced mobile developers can command salaries of $200,000 - per year! That's a princely investment, even for established companies with healthy doses of funding. Hiring an engineer full-time to build your app is a wise long term investment, however we advise against doing so until you have released at least one version of your app and have some traction within the marketplace.

A slightly cheaper option, and probably the best one when

starting out, is to outsource your app development to either an independent app developer, or work with any number of mobile development labs which will build apps for a fixed-price contract. In 2012, an experienced iOS or Android developer, locally based within the USA or Canada, can command hourly rates of roughly $100 /hour. However, we wouldn't recommend working on an hourly basis with a contract engineer to build your app.It's a recipe for sticker shock. A better approach to outsourcing your app development is to push for a fixed-price contract instead of being billed hourly. With a fixed-price contact you agree up front to pay an amount for the app to be built and delivered to the marketplace. The benefit of the fixed-price contract is the price transparency and alignment of incentives with your engineer. With a fixed-price contract, you eliminate the possibility of unforeseen complications and delays eating up your funding. Software development is a time-intensive process, and you want your developer spending the time ironing out all of the issues and bugs that arise without worry for how much that is costing you. Remember the commandment: your development timeline will slip, your app will be delayed getting to the market; be prepared for this eventuality by working with contract developers on a fixed-price contract.

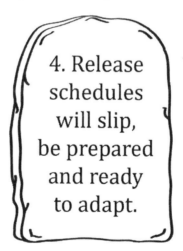

4. Release schedules will slip, be prepared and ready to adapt.

Figure 20: Use fixed-price contracts for contract engineering to keep unforeseen bugs from eating up your funding

- **Independent Developers vs. Development Labs**

When you outsource your engineering you can either work with independent engineers or with mobile development labs that have their own developers and offer contract engineering as a service. When working with independent engineers, you are going to play a much more direct management function than working via a development lab. With development labs you are typically assigned a Project Manager (PM) who works with you to understand your requirements, and in turn manages their team of engineers to get it built. You generally don't interact with the engineers, as the PM is responsible for the management of the effort. The benefit of this type of arrangement is that you do not need to worry about managing programmers and can instead focus on the business side of your app. However, when you work with mobile development labs, you are more likely to pay more than you would with independent engineers. The larger the development lab, the more likely you will be quoted an inflated price as you will be paying for their overhead costs, in addition to the Project Manager and whomever else that is staffed on your project.

- **Local vs. Offshore**

One of the great differentiators in the cost to build your app will be the location of your engineers. Generally, North American based engineers will command much higher hourly rates than developers based in India and Eastern Europe. When looking at offshore development labs, you can expect to pay around $15 - $20 /hour for a junior mobile engineer. The cost differential is non-trivial, and moving to an offshore development team lowers the cost for you to initially develop your app. However, offshoring your development comes with very real risks that you will need to measure the economic benefits against:

- **Time-zones**

If you are US-based and are working with Indian or Chinese developers, you are dealing with 10-12 hour time zone differences. When you are sleeping is when your developers will be working and vice versa. This disconnection due to time zone difference is a very real challenge when creating an app as it will significantly slow down your progress. For every issue or question that a developer has, they will probably need to wait a full day before you are able to respond and direct them. Not only will this burn time, but if you are paying on a per-hour basis this will eat into it too. If you do decide to offshore your development, South American countries like Brazil and Argentina offer competitive developer rates (~$25 /hour) with the added benefit of having a closer time difference.

- **Quality**
When considering off shore development, remember the 9th Appster commandment: You get what you pay for when it comes to engineers and designers. Many of the outsourcing shops you will work in India are veritable app factories, with each developer being assigned to multiple different projects at a single time. While you may only pay $15 /hour for their work, you might end up with an app that is buggy or in the worst case doesn't work. When looking at offshore development labs, try to find those that have a portfolio of work that they've done on other apps. Download and try those apps out. The quality of the work you see in them is likely to be the quality of work your app will receive.

- **Cultural Differences**
A common thread we hear from people who have had bad experiences working with offshore development teams are the cultural and communication barriers that separate North American customers and their off-shore developers. Ask anyone who has managed an international team at a corporation and they'll tell you the difficulty that can arise from cultural differences in a team.

For instance, when working with Indian development teams, be prepared to hear them say 'yes' to a request of yours only to find later that it wasn't done. This isn't because the developers are lazy, but rather they didn't know how to do something or didn't quite understand the requirement but still said 'yes' out of a cultural norm to do so. Unless you've had that experience before, you are liable to get a rude shock when you thought something would have been done but it wasn't.

Another area where cultural differences can impact your app development is in visual layouts and color. Unless you exactly specify every color and shape in your app, the developer is going to use his or her own judgment when creating your app. They might choose colors and layouts that seem to work well to them, but which are awkward and unsightly to you.

The greater the cultural gap between you and your development team, the more likely it is your app will be delayed or turn out not quite right because of simple misunderstandings. If you are building a social networking app, then building it requires a developer to understand how users will use the app. Furthermore, the look and feel of the app needs to be conducive for whatever social interactions the app is fostering. It's possible that the app built for you will be functionally complete, but its user experience could suffer if the developer doesn't have the necessary cultural awareness to make the right feature decisions.

In the end, the more involved you are willing to be to manage your development effort, the less it will cost and the better the final result. While writing code is a highly skilled function that we do not recommend you to learn, managing a project team is not. More so, if you are managing your development team, you will see your app being built in front of your eyes. The more people that are between you and those writing your code, the more warped the final product will be. As the commandment states, your specs and prototypes will become outdated the second code starts to be written. You will see things that do not work as well you thought, and you will see new ways to improve your app. If you are directly involved in the day to day engineering effort, you are much better positioned to identify issues and react to them.

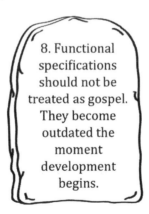

8. Functional specifications should not be treated as gospel. They become outdated the moment development begins.

Figure 21: When you manage your own project, you will be able to make course-corrections as your app is developed

Developer Quotes: No Two Will be the Same

One thing you will notice once you have gotten a few quotes for building your app is that no two will be the same price. In fact, the variability in the price quoted for your app will be huge, ranging from the low-thousands all the way up to the hundreds of thousands of dollars. No, they aren't necessarily trying to scam you; the reality of software development is that it's very difficult to make accurate estimates. Building an app is not like building a house. There is little standardization and every app will be different than the last one that an engineer has built.

When you talk to two different vendors, you can expect two wildly different quotes because they each have their own idea of how to build it and their own estimation of how long it will take. Further, you will realize that the developers who quote you low-ball amounts to build an app usually have a greatly exaggerated sense of how quickly they can turn build your app. It may be tempting to go with an independent developer who gives you the lowest estimate, but you are probably walking into a situation where the engineer either underestimates the work that is involved or is overconfident in their ability to execute on it. On the other hand, if you work with a large mobile development lab, you can expect to be quoted prices that can reach into the hundreds of thousands of dollars. You will also need to take these quotes with a rather large dosage of salt, as these labs are liable to staff your project with testers, project managers, and documentation writers, all of whom need to be paid. These larger shops provide you with the security of very well built products, but you *will* pay for them!

Face it: you aren't building a deck, you are building an app. The quotes you get from engineers and development labs are not much more than wild-ass guesses made by them. To help you get quotes that can be meaningfully compared with each other, here are a few tips to help:

- **Be consistent in how you describe your app**
Describe what you are trying to build in the exact same way to every engineer. Words count here, and even the slightest change in the way you describe a feature to someone can skew the cost estimate. Write down your 'pitch' to developers and make sure you deliver it the same way to everyone you are asking for a quote

from.

• Ask for un-buffered estimates of time to complete

Buffering is a software engineering term to describe inserting a cushion of time to handle unexpected issues and bugs that might crop up during development. Some engineers insert buffers into their quotes, others don't. When asking for a quote, make sure they are not inserting buffer time into their estimate. Instead, you should ask for un-buffered estimates, determine an appropriate buffer multiple, and then multiply each quote by the same factor to come up with a realistic time-to-complete that is standardized across vendors.

• Use mockups!

When it comes to describing your app, a picture is easily worth a thousand words. The more you can show via a mockup or prototype of what you want your app to look and feel like, the less that is left up to the imagination of the engineer. If you can build a mockup that shows a realistic experience for your app, you are taking a lot of the guesswork and fudge factor that an engineer has to do when coming up with an estimate.

• So How Much Does it Cost to Get an App Built?

Just like most questions asked in life, the answer is: it depends. The cost of building your app is going to be directly proportional to the size and complexity of your app.

Complexity is hard to quantify, but generally the more your app does in terms of web communication, social interaction, location monitoring and media streaming, the more complex it is for a developer to build it. In general, the simplest app (imagine a basic utility app, with no internet connectivity) will cost about $5,000 - $10,000 to ship. As you increase the scope of your app to include custom graphics, more screens, Internet connectivity and social networking features, the price moves up. It's not uncommon for a fully-fledged social networking app to cost up to $100,000 and require multiple engineers to complete.

If you are on a tight budget, then simplicity is the key thing to remember to keep your engineering costs low. Even the smallest sacrifice in terms of user experience and functionality can yield enormous savings in engineering. Here are a few tips to keep your engineering costs down:

- **Reduce the number of screens**
Each distinct screen in your app comes with a cost in terms of development and testing. The most basic screen still requires your designer to create graphics for it and for the developer to wire it up within your application. Look at your app, eliminate unnecessary screens and consolidate them down to a very basic set. Reuse the same wizards and detail and list screens across your app as much as possible.

- **Use out-of-box controls, graphics and fonts**
Each major mobile operating system comes with a standard set of UI controls (buttons, checkboxes, lists, etc.), graphics and fonts. When designing your app, try to use as many standard controls and fonts as possible. By sticking to what the operating system provides, you eliminate the need for a designer to create custom graphics and for the developer to work on how to display them across devices. The downside is that your app might look a little plain, but your wallet will be thicker because of it. (You can always change this on a later iteration once you've gained some traction.)

- **Choose a small set of devices and operating system versions to support**
As much as the mobile platforms will lead you to believe that you can build your app once and have it run across an entire gamut of devices (i.e., Android), this is rarely ever the case. For your app, pick a small set of devices (i.e., HTC Inspire, Samsung Galaxy, etc.) and operating system versions (i.e. iOS 5.1, Android 4.0) to support. The fewer devices and operating system versions you will support on your app, the less hacking your engineer will need to get your app to run the same on all of them.

Every app project is different, and the costs to produce them will vary. However, based on our experience, apps generally fall into the following price ranges (U.S.-based developers):

App Type	Example	Estimated Price (USD)
Utility – standalone, with no internet connectivity	Frequent flier management app (i.e. C-Life)	~ $10,000
Informational – internet connected	RSS readers (i.e. Feedler)	~ $10,000 – $20,000
Utility – internet connected	Yelp, Urbanspoon, TweetDeck	~ $15,000 - $50,000
Social Networking	Pinterest, Path	~ $25,000 - $75,000
Location-based Social Networking	Highlight, Sonar	~ $50,000 - $100,000

Figure 22: General price ranges of certain apps (sampled from 4 independent development labs)

These costs are substantially higher than what you might be quoted from an offshore development lab. However, as we mentioned earlier, there are risks that come from offshoring your development that you need to weigh against these amounts.

Hosting

If your app has a server backend that it communicates with through the Internet, you will need to make it available to your app through the Internet. This is called *hosting*. With hosting, you are paying a third-party vendor to run the backend components of your app on a machine that they own and that is accessible through the Internet.

For instance, if you are building a messaging app that allows people to send text messages to each other, you will have a central server and database that the app communicates with to send and receive messages. This server and database needs to be accessible to the app over the Internet and with sufficient speed such that the app doesn't feel slow when sending or receiving messages.

Your hosting costs will depend on the hosting provider, the amount of traffic coming to and from the server, and the number servers that are created to support your app (i.e. you may have one server located in North America and one in Asia to support users of your app in different geographical areas).

Hosting comes in all sorts of different flavors, but the two most important hosting options for app developers to know about are Cloud Hosting and Fixed Hosting.

Cloud Hosting

Not since 'dot com' popped into the common vernacular has a term been thrown around with such reckless abandon as the 'cloud'. *Cloud Hosting* is a fancy name for a rapidly growing hosting model that provides customers with an elastic set of resources that is billed based on usage. Amazon's EC2, Microsoft's Windows Azure and Google's App Engine are all examples of cloud hosting options you can use to host your server and database.

The benefit of cloud hosting is that you can add and remove resources dedicated to your server based on customer demand. So if your messaging app gets popular, the strain on your server will increase and you would add additional CPU and hard drive resources to meet demand. On the flip side, if your app traffic dwindles, you can remove additional resources to match the reduced demand.

Further, with cloud hosting you are able to load-balance traffic coming to your server across multiple servers, which may be distributed across the world without physically needing to purchase the additional hardware. With cloud hosting, if your messaging app is being used in India, then you can very easily create an additional instance of your server located in an Indian datacenter. The actual provisioning of that server and all associated tasks to get it up and running in the Indian data center is handled by your cloud hosting provider.

It's hard to deny the appeal of the cloud-hosting model, as it eliminates the need for you to maintain the staff and hardware to maintain your server and database infrastructure. However, the economics of the cloud only become beneficial when you actually need the elastic resourcing provided by the cloud.

Cloud hosting is billed on a usage basis, which is usually measured in terms of CPU time, bandwidth transferred or hard disk space used. For an app that is just starting out, it can actually be more expensive to host it on a cloud provider versus a more traditional Fixed hosting option.

Fixed Hosting

While cloud hosting providers model themselves like a utility, the more traditional types of hosting, which we refer to as *Fixed Hosting*, provides a static set of resources for a fixed dollar amount. Fixed hosting doesn't come with the ability to dynamically add or remove resources for your server, and often limits you to a single instance of your server and database running on a machine shared with other customers. When you are starting out with your app, a fixed-price hosting plan is usually cheaper than cloud hosting.

However, the downsides associated with fixed hosting are that your server will not be able to respond to increased load or expanded geographic usage like a cloud-hosted option would. If you are creating a messaging app, then with your server on a fixed-hosting plan, users will notice slowdown in service as more people use the app, and users in foreign countries will be plagued with more delays as the geographical distance between them and the server increase waiting times.

Ultimately, if your app gains traction, then you will be best served by a cloud-hosting plan. However, when your app is new and you have few users, the costs of elastic hosting are much higher than fixed hosting. With Fixed hosting you can expect to pay anywhere from $5 /month and up while Cloud hosting plans usually begin at around $50 /month.

In general, we recommend that apps from the very beginning be engineered to operate in cloud-hosted environments but to be hosted on a cheaper, fixed-hosting plan. As the app scales and becomes more established, you can then make the switch to cloud hosting. However, until your app has shown itself to require the scalability and geographical reach provided by cloud hosting, a fixed-hosting plan can provide you with an economical alternative.

Domain Registration

If you are looking to build a web presence for your app, like a marketing web site, you will need to reserve a web address that people can use to find it. The process of finding and reserving a web address is often referred to as *domain registration*. It's fairly simple and cheap to reserve a domain online through marketplaces such as GoDaddy and HostGator. Reserving a .com address can cost as little as $9.99 for 2 years. The price you pay for reserving a domain depends on the popularity of the name you selected and the domain suffix (i.e., *.com*, *.net*, *.ca*, etc.) you picked for it.

You'll find most commonly spelled English words combined with *.com* or *.net* are already taken. If you have a name you really want to use for your app, but its *.com* address is taken, you just need to be a little clever to snag another equally effective web address. A common trend in recent years is for web sites to use less commonly used domain suffixes such as *.ly* in lieu of the much more commonly used *.com* (i.e., Bitly uses *bit.ly* as its URL). If a *.ly* address doesn't work for you, you can try to take your app name and find a domain suffix for a country that matches the last two characters of your app name (i.e., Gabon's domain suffix is *.ga*, if you can come up with a name of your app that ends in 'ga', you could use a *.ga* URL for it)

If you must have the *.com* address and it is already taken, your last option is to contact the current owner of that domain and offer to buy it from them. You can use a free online tool called WHOIS to find out the domain registration for any address. This tool will return contact information for whoever is listed as the current owner of that domain.

Marketplace Commissions

Selling an app through an app marketplace isn't free. For the major app marketplaces like the Apple App Store and Google Play, you will pay a 30% commission to the marketplace on every sale you make. If your app is free, than you pay nothing. Currently, the defacto standard for commissions on app sales is 30%. If you are selling your app for $0.99, then for each sale you will receive ~$0.70 in your pocket. This commission extends beyond the sale of the app to each freemium or in-app purchase made.

Marketplace	Commission
Apple App Store	30%
Google Play	30%
Windows Store	30%

Figure 23: App marketplace commissions by platform

4.3

Monetizing Dani's List

We have a few different options when we look at monetizing Dani's List: we could charge for the app, we can include *freemium* functionality, or we can make it ad-revenue supported. However, even though Dani's List has a utility aspect to it, we should avoid the temptation of charging money for it. The reason is simple: Dani's List relies on crowdsourcing activities from its users and thus is more of social networking concept than pure utility. To be effective, crowdsourcing requires a high volume of users using the app and contributing activities. Thus, while charging \$0.99 would likely yield us some revenue from people trying out the app, we would likely not achieve the density of users to have the app be useful to people. A better approach would be to list Dani's List as a free app and introduce revenue streams through either advertising or freemium functionality.

Display Advertising

Display advertising is the most straightforward way we can monetize Dani's List. We could reserve the bottom or top portion of our app to display advertisements mediated through a third-party service. It is likely that we can achieve higher CPC/CPM rates than normal by the fact that our app is a location based app. Since Dani's List is about finding activities near to the user, we can feed the location data of the user to the ad network, which can then in turn display ads which are more geographically relevant to the user. The higher revenue is due to the increased probability of the user of the app clicking on an advertisement for something that is near to them, than of some randomly selected advertisement. Since Dani's List is meant to be a free app, including some display advertisement into the UI is a good idea. However, display advertising will only start to yield noteworthy revenue once Dani's

List has grown to the tens of thousands of users. Until then, we should also look at other avenues for revenue potential.

Content Advertising

Dani's List offers an interesting opportunity for monetization through sponsored activities within the app. As we mentioned earlier in the chapter, content advertising is the introduction of sponsored content within the app. As Dani's List is all about helping people find interesting things to do around them, it's likely that local business would be interested in promoting activities that include them. However, it is not realistic for us to build content advertising into the first versions of Dani's List, as the technical cost of investing in purchasing platform for potential advertisers to advertise within the app far out weight the likely revenues that could be achieved. However, if Dani's List is able to achieve significant user scale in the longer term, then content advertising can turn into a formidable revenue engine for the app in lieu of display advertising.

'Freemium'

In-app purchases, or *freemium* as the industry likes to call it, offers numerous avenues for revenue generation outside of display advertisements. The concept of freemium relies on creating hooks (virtual goods, additional features, etc.) within the app that would entice users to buy. The hooks themselves can be anything we want, but in order to generate revenue they need to be something a user would conceivably want to purchase.

Since Dani's List is primarily a utility app, there isn't much of an avenue for creating virtual currencies or selling virtual goods within the app. Instead, our freemium strategy will rely on offering two different versions of the app: a free version and a paid one.

Most users will initially start with the free version, and our goal would be to create enough of an incentive from using it that users will want to upgrade to the paid version at a later point. However, this means we need to introduce enough enhanced functionality in the paid version to create a real incentive to upgrade. Here are a few ideas for some premium functionality we can provide:

- Remove all display advertising in premium version. Many users find display advertisements annoying, as they take up space and clutter the experience. Within the app we can display to the user that they can remove all ads by upgrading to the premium version.

- Limit the number of activities a user can add to their personal list in the free version. It is likely when a user starts to use Dani's List, they will only have a few items on their list. As they use the app more, they will likely increase the number of items they have on it. We can monetize Dani's List by capping the number of free activities a person can add to ten. Once a user reaches that limit they won't be able to add any more until they complete one of the activities or upgrade.

- Allow users to share their lists with friends only when they use the premium version. It's likely that users would want to collaboratively work on lists with their friends, and this offers another avenue to introduce a purchasing point.

- Allow users to view their lists on the web or on another device only in the premium version of the app.

With this list alone, it's likely we can entice some subset of the free users of the app to upgrade to the premium version. The premium version of the app can be offered at a typical one-time purchase amount of $0.99. While it's likely we will offer the premium version for an up-front purchase price of $0.99 at the start, the long-term goal for the premium version is to eventually move to a subscription based model. With subscriptions, the user would need to essentially re-purchase the app every month to continue to use the premium functionality. However, let's not put the horse before the cart. A subscription model requires having an app that people would be willing to subscribe to. Dani's List may eventually get there, but to start, we'll look to market the premium version for a flat $0.99.

5

Understanding App Technology

So we come to it at last, the section of the book devoted to mobile app technology. If you are new to the tech world, then you might be mystified and intimidated by the endless stream of acronyms and jargon that gets thrown around when people talk technology. Relax., You don't need to be a techno wizard to understand the mechanics behind a mobile app, and you don't need to learn how to code.

In this chapter, we will peel back the onion and give you a basic rundown of the technology behind mobile apps. By the end of the chapter, you will have a good understanding of the different mobile platforms and components that come together, both on the phone and on the web, to bring a mobile app to life.

While it's not critical that you learn the nitty-gritty technical details, it is very important that you become literate in mobile app technology. Even a rudimentary knowledge of the technology will allow you to communicate with your engineers and understand the various issues that are bound to crop out while your app is built.

If you are managing a team of engineers, then you need to be able to ask informed questions and be conversant on the technical aspects of the project. Otherwise you will be completely at the mercy of your engineers. While this might not sound like a bad thing, let me assure you - it is. You are the owner of your app. *You* hold the vision of what it's meant to become, not your engineers. The decisions your engineers make will not always align with what is right for your app from a business perspective. If you can't have a technical conversation with your engineers, they will ignore your ideas and do things the way they think is best.

5.1

The Appster Dilemma: Native vs. Mobile Web Apps?

When you set out to build a mobile app, one of the first things you will need to decide is just what kind of app to build. Should you build an app for the iPhone? What about Android? Should you forego a native app and bet it all on a HTML-based web app? These are all fundamental decisions you will need to make before building you can build an app. Once you decide to build a certain type of app on a particular platform, you are locked into that choice.

Recall from Chapter 2 that there are broadly two different types of mobiles apps: native apps vs. mobile web apps. A native app is one that you download from a marketplace like the Apple App Store and run directly atop your smartphone's operating system. On the other hand are mobile web apps which are websites that run inside a mobile browser, more popularly referred to as *HTML5* apps. A mobile web app is simply a web site that has been styled to fit the smaller screen of a smartphone. With the advent of HTML5, the latest version of the venerable web-browsing standard, mobile web apps can now replicate much of what previously could only be done by a native app.

The first technology decision you will face is whether to build a mobile web app or a native app. If you've decided that your app must be available to both Android and iOS and you are willing to live with the limitations provided by a browser-based app, then you might lean towards building a mobile web app. If you are building a photo-sharing app that you are looking to monetize with direct downloads and freemium functionality, then you might consider building a native app. However, before you do let us introduce another type of app that lies somewhere in between a pure mobile web app and a native app: the hybrid app.

Hybrid Apps

There is a middle ground between native apps and mobile web apps. They are called *hybrid* apps. As the name suggests, a hybrid app combines functionality of native apps with the platform independence of mobile web apps. A hybrid app is, in reality, a native app that serves as a thin container for a mobile web app written in HTML & JavaScript. Unlike a mobile web app, a hybrid app does not run in a browser, but instead as its own native app. Since a hybrid app runs as a native app, it can access all of the capabilities of the smartphone. However, unlike a native app, all of the logic of the app is written in HTML & JavaScript. Thus, with a hybrid app, you would write the app much like a regular mobile web app; however, since the HTML doesn't run inside of a browser, the app can leverage the phone's hardware just like a native app.

A hybrid app's main advantage over a purely native app is that HTML allows it to be rendered on any modern smartphone without needing to be completely re-written. To create a version of the app that can run on a different platform, all that would need to be done is create the native app for that platform, which will host all of the same HTML & JavaScript of the app.

However, hybrid apps are no panacea and do come with their own disadvantages. For one, a hybrid app still needs to be downloaded and installed through an app marketplace. Furthermore, a hybrid app requires a separate middleware technology to serve as the native app container to the HTML & JavaScript. This middleware is what provides the native container that renders a hybrid app's HTML & JavaScript logic.

The Apache Cordova framework (formerly known as PhoneGap) is the most popular and widely used of these hybrid frameworks. To write a hybrid app using Apache Cordova, your developer would need to be familiar with the various APIs and other hooks introduced by Cordova to get access to location services and the phone's camera. This introduces a technical wrinkle since your hybrid app code relies on a third party framework in order to run. This reliance on an external framework can introduce bugs and complications to your development schedule. For instance if a bug crops up in your app such that it is unable to get a GPS position fix, your developer will need to diagnose whether the bug is caused by the underlying phone platform, the middleware framework or in the app code itself. Furthermore, your development schedule can be put in jeopardy by the lack of documentation on the part of the middleware framework.

Finally, while hybrid apps do provide considerable advantages over a mobile web app, they still do not match a native app in performance. Hybrid apps faced a huge setback in the summer of 2012 when Facebook announced it was abandoning its hybrid app for a pure native app. Facebook's mobile app customers had long complained about the poor responsiveness of the app's UI and other bugs that accompanied it. Clicking buttons within the old hybrid app often didn't work, and when they did, they did so with a considerable lag. These performance issues are inherent to any app written in HTML & JavaScript, be it a plain mobile web app or a hybrid app. On the other hand, since a native app runs directly on the phone's hardware (unlike HTML which must be rendered by a browser or a native app container) its UI will almost always be more responsive than a web or hybrid app. These performance issues limit the applicability of mobile web and hybrid approaches to apps that are consumptive in nature with limited user interaction, such as a cookbook or news reading app.

	Advantages	Disadvantages	Good For
Native Apps	• Speed, run much faster than web apps. • Do not require an internet connection to use. • Can access smartphone hardware, such as GPS, music player and camera.	• Costly to develop, typical app takes 3-6 months to build. • Requires specialized developer skill set. • Runs only on single platform.	• Photo sharing or location based apps (i.e., Instagram, Highlight). • Graphic intensive gaming. • Media playing apps (i.e. Spotify)
Web Apps	• Can be used on any device with a modern web browser.	• Requires an internet connection to be used.	• Newspaper, information sharing apps (i.e., Financial Times)

• Does not require user to download app from marketplace. • Can easily adapt existing web site to be mobile ready. • Easier to find a web developer than a platform developer.	• Cannot access GPS, or camera. • Cannot receive push notifications. • Has to be run within a web browser.	• Cookbooks, restaurant guides. • Building mobile experiences around websites.

Figure 24: Comparison of Mobile Web Apps vs. Native Apps

5.2

Choosing Your Mobile Platform

If you go down the path of a native app, then you need to choose which mobile platform to build upon. The word *platform* refers to the mobile operating system that the app is designed to run on. In smartphone land, there are three major mobile platforms to choose from: Apple's iOS (e.g., the iPhone/iPad), Google's Android (e.g., Samsung Galaxy), and Microsoft's Windows Phone (e.g., Nokia Lumia). Apps written for iOS will not run upon Android or Windows, and vice versa.

Furthermore, porting an app from one platform to the next requires a complete re-write of the code. So depending on what you are building, who your audience is, and how you aim to monetize your app, you need to carefully choose which platform to build on as it is very difficult and costly to change later on.

Android vs. iOS: Market Share vs. App Revenue

Google's Android and Apple's iOS are the two giants in the smartphone marketplace with Android claiming 56percent of worldwide market share and iOS 23 percent.[14] Even though Android is the market leader, these market share numbers obfuscate the reality that Android users are not likely to pay for apps, especially when compared to iPhone users. In 2011, iOS claimed 85percent of all global app revenue[15], with roughly $3.5 billion in revenue collected by app developers[16], compared to $340 million for Android developers[17]. If your monetization strategy depends on users paying for your app, or through in-app purchases (i.e. freemium), then iOS is by far the more lucrative option.

However, if you are building a free app and are looking to generate revenue through advertising, the Android platform becomes more attractive as you are likely to have a greater audience to tap into due to its much more expansive device footprint.

Nevertheless, even with display advertising, you are likely to receive smaller CPC and CPM rates on Android than a comparable app built on iOS. A 2012 study by Opera Software found that the average CPM on an iOS app to be $1.64 versus $0.88 on Android.[23]

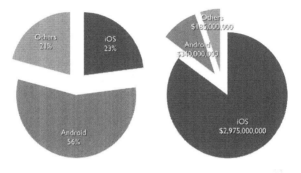

Figure 25: Platform market share vs. App Revenue

Flexibility: Android's Gift and Curse

Unlike iOS, Android is an open platform that allows developers to build apps that replace the keyboard or introduce completely new UI shells, both of which are impossible to do in iOS. Furthermore, prior to release, every iOS app must be reviewed and approved by Apple, which has a somewhat arbitrarily enforced set of guidelines that commonly rejects apps for being 'potentially offensive' or for not following Apple UI design guidelines. On the other hand, Google Play (the Android app marketplace) allows developers to publish apps with very little review done by Google. For instance, building a photo-sharing app on Android will require less work than on iOS because Apple guidelines require it to include content moderation functionality.

Yet, this flexibility is at the root of the problems with Android. At a technical level, it's much easier to develop a high-quality app on iOS than it is Android. On iOS, you are only building an app to run on a small set of Apple-built devices that for the most part run the latest version of Apple's iOS. Android, though, is designed to run atop hundreds of different devices, with very few of them actually manufactured by Google. Furthermore, the Android landscape is fragmented by the different versions of the Android operating system. As of November 2012, only about 40 percent[24] of Android devices were running the latest version of Android (version 4.0, codenamed 'Ice Cream Sandwich,' and version 4.1, codenamed Jelly Bean, combined) compared to nearly 73 percent[20] for the latest iOS (versions 6 and 6.1, combined). This fragmentation causes real problems, as each phone introduces its own idiosyncrasies in how Android behaves atop of it. This makes it extremely difficult to build an app that will run smoothly across different Android devices and operating system versions. If you do choose Android, have some sympathy for your developer, and make sure to clearly specify which Android devices and specific versions that you want to support.

Windows Phone: Because 3rd Place Isn't So Bad

The dark horse of mobile platforms is Microsoft's Windows Phone. While it's 2.6 percent market-share[18] is tiny, and its app store relatively small (~125,000 apps)[19], the Windows Phone has received critical acclaim for its design and stands to benefit from Nokia's adoption for use in all future smartphones. The small number of apps on the Windows Phone Marketplace provides the last green-field opportunity for app developers to build apps with little competition in categories that have long-since been flooded in the App Store and Google Play (there is currently still no Instagram app for Windows).

One great benefit of Windows Phone is its continued integration with Microsoft's full-stack of IT products. This makes Windows Phone particularly well suited for deployment in enterprise environments. Thus, if you are building a business-to-business (B2B) app or one designed for enterprise users, Windows Phone is a good place to start. In late 2012, Microsoft introduced a substantial update to Windows Phone with the release of Windows Phone 8 which further integrated Windows Phone into corporate IT management infrastructures.

One shouldn't confuse building a mobile app to immediately mean that you should build a native app on any of the three major mobile platforms. If you do not need to use the camera or GPS of the smartphone, or you are building an app that is designed for information consumption rather than user interaction, then we recommend that you consider a mobile web or hybrid app, which will immediately bring your app to any smartphone platforms and avoid the heavy investment required to build a native app.

However, if you do choose the path of a native app, we prefer the iOS and Windows platforms, as they provide both a superior development experience and increased revenue opportunities that make them a more attractive of a choice than Android.

	Advantages	Disadvantages	Good For
Apple iOS	• Accounts for 85% of all global app revenue. • User base more engaged in 'app culture'. • Easy to build high-quality apps with Apple-built hardware.	• Apple's app review policy is stringent and arbitrarily enforced. • Platform limits what apps can do. • Highly competitive app marketplace.	• Pay-to-download and 'freemium' apps. • Location-based discovery apps (require high density urban environments) • Niche targeted app ideas.
Google Android	• Open platform allows you to build a wider variety of apps. • Quick and easy to ship an app to Google Play due to light review process. • Full-integration with Google services.	• Device fragmentation makes it difficult to build for multiple phones. • Poor development tools. • Little app revenue generated by users. • Highly competitive marketplace.	• Graphics-intensive gaming. • Mass-market communication apps. • Free-to-download, ad-revenue supported app concepts.
Microsoft Windows Phone	• Very little competition in popular app categories.	• Very small install user base. • Takes a long time to ship due	• Enterprise apps.

• Financial incentives from Microsoft. • Well-suited for enterprise app scenarios. • Easy to find qualified developer talent.	to stringent app review process. • Primitive reporting tools to monitor app sales.	

Figure 26: Comparison of the 3 major mobile platforms

5.3

App Anatomy: What is an App Made of?

While the term *app* refers to what the user interacts with on their smartphone, most apps are actually comprised of different components that come together to form the entire app. Depending on the type of app you are building, you might need to build separate components, such as back end servers, databases and web sites, in addition to the app that runs on the phone. So if you are building a simple utility app, like an alarm clock, then the only component that needs to be built is the native app that will be downloaded and installed from the marketplace. However, if you wanted to include functionality that allows a user to stream a radio station for their alarm, or to manage their alarms through a web site, then your app will also require back end components, such as a web site, a web server and database to work. Generally if your app is going to store and retrieve data from the web, you will likely need to build additional back-end components that will live on the web and be accessible from the phone. The exception to this rule is if your app will be plugging into existing online services, like Google maps or Facebook, then you can use capabilities within the mobile platform to plug into these services without needing to build any back-end components.

Before we confuse you too much with esoteric component names, here are descriptions of common app components and how they work together:

Component	Description
App	• Software that typically lives on the phone and serves as the main interface for your users. • "Native" apps are downloaded and installed on the phone. • "Mobile Web" apps are run within the browser on the phone.
Website	• Websites are typically used to provide marketing and support information for users downloading your app.

	• Websites are also used to enable sharing of content from the app to Facebook, Twitter etc. For example, when you click on a photo shared from Instagram on Facebook, you are directed to the Instagram website where you are able to view the photo.
Server	• Servers are kind of like a web site, except instead of displaying content for people to view, a server returns content for the app to consume. • Apps communicate with a Server through the Internet and use the Server to store and retrieve data. For example, when you upload a picture to Facebook using a mobile app, the app is sending data to a Facebook Server that saves it in a Database and makes it available for other people with the App to see. • Servers act as the intermediary between the App and the Database where all data is stored. • Servers are generally custom built components designed to support the functionality of the mobile app. A well designed Server can support apps that run across all platforms along with providing data to support any web sites.
Database	• The Database is where all data sent to your Server is permanently stored. Think of the Database as a giant warehouse that holds the data of your App. • The Server uses the Database to store and retrieve data sent to it by the App. If the Database is the warehouse, then the Server is like the window agent that takes requests for data and instructs the Database to retrieve it.

Figure 27: Technical components that can form a single app

(Note: This taxonomy is not by any means standardized and you might find some of the terms like *database* and *server* to mean different things depending on who you ask. For the sake of our book and to keep this as simple as possible, we've purposely simplified the model.)

Anatomy of a Native App

As we've discussed, a native app is downloaded from a

marketplace, and installed locally on the smartphone. Thus the app component from the previous table refers to the code written atop the mobile operating system that lives and runs on the smartphone. Data that an app needs to run is stored locally on the phone. Apps that require data to be stored on the web use the mobile operating system to interact with a backend server and database via the Internet.

Anatomy of a Mobile Web App

Mobile web apps are actually web sites designed to be accessible from the web browser of a smartphone. The app component from the previous table refers to a web site that a user visits with their mobile web browser. A mobile web app might also require a separate web site viewable from a laptop for support, marketing and social media sharing. Depending on the user experience of your app, you can sometimes leverage the same code in the mobile web site for the more general-purpose site. As mobile web apps live on the web, all data that they store will need to be held in a central database component that the web site will be built on. For example, if you were building a news reader as a mobile web app, the web site code would pull news articles out of the database and display them to the user in their browser. In general, a web based mobile app will not require a separate server component independent of the web site, as all logic for the app itself is run through the web site.

5.4

Choosing the Right Technology: Looking Beyond the Jargon

People in the tech world love using esoteric acronyms and impenetrable jargon, perhaps as a way to make themselves sound smarter or maybe just to confuse others. The next time you go to a tech Meetup, try asking someone, "What technology should I use to build my mobile app?" You should probably bring an umbrella with you because you will be drenched in a torrent of technological jargon. You might feel overwhelmed by it all, but do not let it get you down! The secret truth about technology is that so many of the acronyms you hear are describing different ways to do the same thing. If you understand the meaning behind one piece of jargon, chances are you understand the meaning of countless others.

If you decide that you will also need a server and database for your app, then you will need to choose which technology to use to build each of those components. Just like a contractor chooses between aluminum and wood to use for the framing of a house, you will need to pick the materials your team will use to build each component. If you have a technical cofounder, you can generally leave it up to them to choose the technology. However, if you don't have one, then you should know enough about each of the options to make sure you choose the right technology for the long-term growth of your app and business. Over the coming pages, we will look to demystify the most common of mobile tech jargon and give you some context as to how these various pieces fit together in the process of building an app.

App Technology

If you are building a native app, then your choice of mobile platform will largely dictate the language and tools you will use to build your app.

Mobile Platform	Framework	Language
iOS	Cocoa	Objective-C
Android	Android SDK	JAVA
Windows Phone	.NET	C# / VB.NET

Figure 28: Mobile frameworks and languages by platform

A *language* is the programming syntax used to write the code for your mobile app. The framework is the set of tools written for a specific language that a developer uses to put together the app. Think of a framework as a set of components pre-built in the language of choice that a developer can leverage to create parts of your mobile app. Frameworks make writing code easier because they allow a developer to drop in components that are already pre-built by others instead of having to write everything from scratch.

Thus, if you are looking to build an Android app, you will need to find a software engineer who can program in JAVA and has experience developing with the Android SDK framework. For iOS apps, you will need an engineer that is fluent in the Objective-C language and the Cocoa framework of tools. Finally for Windows Phone apps, you will need an engineer with experience programming in either C# or Visual Basic .NET (VB.NET), using the .NET framework. Generally if an engineer understands the underlying programming language, they should be able to get up to speed using the various frameworks for that language rather quickly.

Server & Web Site Technology

If you are building an app that requires a server or web site component, then you will need to choose which technology should be used to build it. Generally, you should pick a single technology to build both components, as you'll find that many of the technologies listed here can be used to build a server and web site. Remember that a web site is essentially the same as a server except that it renders content for human consumption while a server returns data to a native app running on a phone.

The sheer number of options and acronyms available to you are far greater than can be reasonably contained in these pages, so we will quickly outline a few of them.

ASP.NET MVC

ASP.NET is a web-application framework built by Microsoft that allows developers to create scalable web sites and servers using either the C# or Visual Basic.NET programming language. While older versions of ASP.NET made building robust web applications tedious and time consuming, the latest version, ASP.NET MVC has won acclaim for its simplicity and power. Similar in concept to Ruby-on-Rails (see next page), ASP.NET MVC provides a simple set of patterns that allow a developer to stand up a web site or server in very little time. Using ASP.NET MVC requires you to use Microsoft's .NET framework, and for your web site to be hosted on a machine running Windows. This Windows requirements means you will need to seek out a hosting provider that offers a Windows-based environment and that can run the .NET framework. ASP.NET MVC is an open-source technology released by Microsoft and is free to use. However, ASP.NET MVC is optimized to work against Microsoft's SQL Server database, which requires client licenses and is generally not free.

Node.JS

Node.JS is another framework designed to simplify the process of standing up a web site or server. The key differentiator for Node.JS is that everything from the web site client-code to the code on the back end for the server logic is written in JavaScript. JavaScript is the defacto language for programming web sites within all major web browsers. JavaScript is a very simplified, easy to learn language which trades away the power of JAVA or C# for simplicity and quick development. Node.JS extends the concept of JavaScript beyond web programming to actually include programming the back end logic of a server or web site. The benefit Node.JS brings is that developers who only know JavaScript can now go beyond browser development to build all of the logic of a web site.

The benefit to you of choosing Node.JS is if you have a developer who is proficient in JavaScript, or if you know JavaScript yourself, you can use those skills to build much of the back end of your app. If you are building a mobile Web app, then conceivably you can write all components of your app in JavaScript.

Using Node.JS does come with serious limitations that you should be aware of. JavaScript isn't like Ruby, JAVA or C#. It's a scripting language that doesn't have an ecosystem of frameworks or libraries to complete typical back-end server tasks like communicating with different databases, image processing, etc. This means that when creating the server to support a complex social networking-like app, you will need to write more of the code necessary to complete typical tasks than you would in a more established language like Ruby, or C#, which have a very healthy set of tools and frameworks you can use. Additionally, while Node.JS is a very good choice for building simple web sites, if you are expecting your backend to face heavy traffic and use, it is not well-designed to scale up to handle that traffic. With Frameworks such as ASP.NET MVS and Ruby-on-Rails are designed to be able to scale up to support increased traffic and leverage multiple processors to handle it, while Node.JS isn't.

Ruby-on-Rails

Ruby-on-Rails has exploded in popularity over the past few years as a completely free, open-source framework that enables developers to quickly design and deploy web sites and servers. Built upon the Ruby language, Ruby-on-Rails provides a straightforward set of templates that make standing up a web site largely an exercise in customization, rather than building from scratch (hence the term 'on Rails', as in a guided experience). Like ASP.NET MVC, Ruby-on-Rails is designed to provide a generic framework that can be easily adopted by developers to suit applications of all varieties. You can use Ruby-on-Rails to build both a web site and a server to support your mobile application. Ruby-on-Rails has rocketed in popularity precisely because it takes away much of the painful and tedious coding that was required to build a web site and instead replaces it with configurable options.

The Ruby language is generally considered to be easier for a beginner to learn than JAVA and C++. The emergence of Ruby-on-Rails has lowered the barrier for non-developers to build web sites and servers by making the task of programming them much easier to learn and become proficient on. Given the popularity of Ruby-on-Rails within the startup community, Ruby-on-Rails developers are in very high demand. Go to any tech Meetup and you'll find countless entrepreneurs scouring for anyone who is proficient in Ruby-on-Rails.

You should view Ruby-on-Rails as an equivalent technology to Microsoft ASP.NET MVC. However, unlike ASP.NET MVC, note that Ruby-on-Rails runs atop of the open-source and free MySQL database. Thus with Ruby-on-Rails you will forego the cost of licensing Microsoft SQL Server that would come with ASP.NET MVC.

Database Technology

As we mentioned earlier, think of the database as the warehouse where all of the shared data of your app lives. Depending on the complexity of your app, you might have multiple databases at work, one on the phone itself and another hosted on the Internet to power the web site and server. When picking the database technology to use for your app, you should consider it within the context of the technology you are using to build your server or web site. For instance, if you are looking to build use ASP.NET MVC, then you should probably be using Microsoft's SQL Server as your database as it's designed to fit right into ASP.NET MVC. This doesn't mean you cannot use other database technology with ASP.NET MVC. It's just your developer's life will be much easier if you use them together.

In general, there are two broad types of database technology: SQL databases and NoSQL databases. We won't get too far into the weeds here, but SQL is a language for inserting/modifying and querying data to and from databases. SQL is the defacto standard for manipulating databases and is what powers the most commonly used database technologies such as Oracle, Microsoft SQL Server and MySQL. On the other hand, non-SQL databases take a very different approach to querying databases and look to simplify the process by eliminating many of the complexities that come with SQL. SQL databases are used to power the banks, major web sites, and most large-scale applications on the Internet.

The benefit SQL provides is that it guarantees the consistency of the data while being able to support millions of pieces of data within it. The downside to SQL is that building large-scale web sites and servers atop of it can become difficult when the quantity of data becomes very, very large as performance degrades due to the data consistency guarantees provided by SQL. NoSQL abandons the use of the SQL language, along with the data consistency benefits provided by it, so that large quantities of data can be more easily queried and retrieved. NoSQL is able to achieve this because it does not provide the same guarantees on data consistency that SQL does. Thus, if you are building a web store where users are going to be purchasing or ordering items, data consistency is much more important than if you were building a web site that simply allowed users to share pictures and videos.

Some popular choices for SQL databases are: Microsoft SQL Server, MySQL, Oracle and IBM DB2. Some popular choices for NoSQL databases are Apache CouchDB, Cassandra, Amazon DynamoDB and MongoDB.

Our own experience has taught us to avoid NoSQL databases, only because SQL databases are generally more stable, offer enough performance and have lots of shared knowledge available on the Internet that it leads to quicker development with fewer performance or other scalability issues. You should only consider a NoSQL database if your engineer can show very explicitly why a SQL database will not work for your app. Unless you are building an extremely large-scale app with very unstructured data, you should lean towards picking a SQL database for your backend.

Understanding Stacks

When talking about mobile app technology, a common word you will hear thrown around is *stack*. A stack refers to a collection of tools and frameworks that you can use to build each component of your app. The technology contained within a stack is designed to work together and make the process of building all of the components as seamless as possible. Some stacks contain technologies all built by the same vendor, and others might contain independently built technologies that work together by using the same data formats and behaviors. Not all stacks are created equal. Some might only contain technology for a subset of the components you might need constructed.

Thinking in terms of stacks is an easy way to choose a set of technologies upon which to build your app,while limiting the risk of bugs arising from incompatibilities between them. When you choose a stack, you are leveraging the knowledge and experience of everyone before you that has already built something using it.

LAMP

A popular example of a stack is called LAMP. LAMP is a collection of technology (Linux, Apache, MySQL and PHP) used to build the various components of a website. Linux is the operating system of the machine hosting the web site, Apache is the technology used to make the website accessible to the internet, MySQL is the database used to store all of the site data and PHP is the language in which the web site is written in. LAMP is an open-source stack that means that all of the components are free to use. Ruby-on-Rails and Node.JS are particularly well-suited to the LAMP stack. However, choosing the LAMP stack only gets you part way to building a mobile app. You still need the technology to build an actual native app! Generally, Android and iOS apps have a plethora of open-source libraries available that make communicating with a server built using LAMP simple and painless. On the other hand, if you are building a Windows Phone app, then choosing a server built with LAMP might result in more work and trouble than if you had chosen the Microsoft stack.

Microsoft Windows

The main competitor to LAMP is the Microsoft Windows stack of technology. As you might have guessed, the Microsoft stack contains a set of tools and frameworks, all developed by Microsoft and can build every component of a mobile app. If you were looking to build a Windows Phone app, you'd save yourself a lot of tears and heartache by using Microsoft technology to build the server, database and web site components. The Microsoft stack is made up of the Windows operating system, IIS, ASP.NET MVC, and SQL Server. The great benefit of the Microsoft stack is that it makes building a Windows Phone app painless, as all of the components snap together like they were LEGOs. However, this convenience comes at a cost as the Microsoft technology is not free, and will require you to pay Microsoft for licenses to use Windows and SQL Server.

When you design your app, be aware of what components you might need beyond the app itself. Each additional component will require engineering and testing, and will certainly balloon the cost to develop your app.

5.5

The Tech behind Dani's List

With Dani's List, we need to make some important decisions about the type of app we are planning on building and which platform to build it on. Given that Dani's List is an app that uses both the GPS location and camera of the phone, it makes sense to build a native app (instead of a mobile web or hybrid app). With that decision, we now need to choose the platform to build Dani's List on: Apple's iOS, Google's Android or Microsoft's Windows Phone.

Choosing the Right Mobile Platform

As great of a platform Windows Phone is, its tiny 3 percent market share means that very few people would use Dani's List by virtue of the fact that very few people have a Windows Phone. Building Dani's List on Windows Phone would allow us to tap a possibly underserved market, but it would still preclude Dani's List to achieve any mainstream success.

This leaves us with choosing between iOS or Android. As we mentioned earlier on in the chapter, one of the differentiators between the iOS and Android platforms is the increased propensity for iOS users to purchase apps and freemium content. Android users tend to focus on free apps, leaving Android developers to rely on advertising for a bigger slice of revenue. Furthermore, the location-based nature of Dani's List requires a dense urban environment to grow, most likely New York City or San Francisco, both of which are heavily iOS dominated. The combination of these two factors leads us to build Dani's List upon Apple's iOS platform. Once Dani's List has matured into a final form, that would be the time to make an Android version of the app. Otherwise, we take on the burden of having to maintain two entirely different versions of our app, each of which would need to be changed anytime we changed the app's functionality. As our

Appster commandments tell us that our idea and app will change, especially in the earlier releases, it doesn't make much sense to attempt to build Dani's List for Android at this time. This type of *iOS first* strategy aligns with that of other apps like Foursquare and Instagram.

Even though we've picked iOS we are still not done with platform choices. We now need to choose which versions of iOS to support on Dani's List. Depending on the type of iPhone a person has, they may have a different version of iOS. For example, the iPhone 4 initially shipped with iOS 4.0, the iPhone 4S shipped with iOS 5.0, and the new iPhone 5 comes with iOS 6.0. Users of older iPhones can choose to upgrade their phone to a new version of iOS, or leave their iOS untouched. Each new version of iOS comes with new functionality, making some apps easier to build on iOS 6 than it would on iOS 5. Given that, as of November 2012, about 93percent of iPhone users were running on iOS 5 or later, it makes sense to support Dani's List on iOS 5.0 or higher.[20]

Choosing Server and Database Technology

While Dani's List will exist as a native iOS app, the nature of the app requires a back end server and database component. The need for a server and database component comes from people being able to see other people's activities and add them to their own list. Furthermore, earlier on we mentioned that one of the 'freemium' options with Dani's List would be to make available a user's data through a Dani's List website or even on different device. Both of these require us to store all user data in Dani's List on a centralized server and database that each running instance of the app will pull information from through the Internet.

In addition to a web accessible server and database, Dani's List will need to also have a basic website that anyone can visit from a modern web browser on a laptop. While Dani's List is a mobile app, the ability for users to share their activities on Twitter or Facebook requires a web site that is visible to people on a regular computer. Items that are shared to Twitter or Facebook contain a hyperlink to a website that hosts that content. If someone sees an activity shared by Dani's List on one of their friend's Facebook feed and clicks on it, this link needs to point to a web site that is viewable by someone not on a smartphone.

The technology we choose to build these components is dictated mainly by the expertise of the engineers building the app and their comfort working with different technologies. With Dani's List, the engineers are members of our team at Blue Label Labs and their expertise is in building servers, web sites, and databases using the Microsoft Windows stack. It's a natural choice for us to then use Microsoft stack to put together all three of these components. Given this choice, we will use the following technologies for the back end of Dani's List:

Component	Technology
Server	Windows Communication Foundation (WCF)
Database	SQL Server 2008
Website	ASP.NET MVC

Figure 29: Technologies used in Dani's List

These three technologies are designed to snap together and in general make development fairly straightforward for an experienced Microsoft developer. Finding experienced Microsoft developers isn't difficult, given that these technologies are widely adopted in corporate environments. While ASP.NET MVC and WCF are relatively new technologies, any developer who has experience programming in C# should be able to learn them in very little time.

ASP.NET MVC and WCF are free technologies that can be downloaded straight from the Microsoft Download Center. SQL Server isn't a free product, however there are free version of SQL Server that can be used during the development of your app. When you choose the hosting provider for the server, database and website, you will usually have the option to include a SQL Server database as part of the price of your hosting package.

The Hosting Decision

Once we have our technologies selected, we need to choose

uponwhich company we want to host the backend components of Dani's List. Note that since we've chosen to use the Microsoft stack, we need to find a hosting provider that supports it. If you recall in an earlier chapter, we mentioned two types of hosting: Fixed and Cloud. For applications that have thousands of users geographically spread out across the globe, Cloud hosting is generally the best solution to purchasing additional capacity to support them. However, Dani's List is a brand new app with no user base, and it's likely that the user growth will occur in a geographically condensed area. Thus, going with a Cloud hosting option would be overkill at this point, especially since Microsoft Azure Cloud hosting would cost $50-$100 per month. A better option for Dani's List would be to go with a fixed hosting plan offered by a smaller hosting vendor.

For Dani's List, we chose to host all of the backend components with Winhost. Winhost is a discount hosting provider that hosts Windows based components that also include a Microsoft SQL Server database. For our initial needs with Dani's List, one of Winhost's monthly plans, ranging $5-$20 per month will work fine. Note that by going with Winhost, we have forsaken the elastic capacity provided by Cloud hosting options, like Azure and Amazon EC2. It is likely that as Dani's List grows, we'll need to migrate off of Winhost and onto a Cloud hosting provider.

6

Designing Your App

Designing an app is not like designing a web site or desktop applications. Mobile apps are unique because they are companions to people as they move throughout their day. A regular website doesn't have to think about things like a user abruptly switching away from filling out a form only to come back to complete it some hours later in a totally different context. Websites and desktop applications are easier to design than an app because users are generally sitting down and stationary while interacting with them. Mobile apps rarely ever have the full attention of their user and when they do it's only for seconds at a time. While web sites are consumed in a very constrained environment, mobile apps are used throughout the day as people live their lives. Mobile apps need to be ready to spring into action at any moment and to operate reliably in any number of environments, from subways to a household bathroom. Thus, when it comes to designing an app, you have to build an engaging, entertaining experience that adapts to its user, who could be balancing themselves on a subway train with one hand, and opening your app with the other.

Additionally, mobile apps operate with 2 very important constraints that web sites and desktop applications do not face: battery life and cellular data plan usage. Mobile apps run on a smartphone, and that smartphone has a finite amount of battery life. The task of designing an app is made that much more challenging because you need to minimize both battery drain and the amount of data the app might be pulling down over a metered 3G connection. In this chapter will explore these and other challenges that are inherent in designing a mobile app and offer well-established solutions to overcoming them. Further, we will delve into a discussion of UI metaphors to use in mobile apps, and how to best create an engaging experience on a small screen while keeping the user informed and aware of where they are in your app. Finally, we will take what we've learned up until now and put it to work by designing the UI for the Dani's List app.

6.1

Batteries Don't Last Forever

Logic should tell you that the more work a smartphone does the more power it will draw from its battery. As many people go through their entire day on a single battery charge, the margin for any unusual battery drain is small. If your app consumes significant battery life, your users will notice when they run out of power before they'd normally expect. The more an app does, the longer it runs, the more battery life it consumes.

If you are building an app that simply records information a user inputs into a form, then battery life isn't that much of a concern. However, if you are building a location-aware app, such as Highlight, which needs to constantly keep track of where the user is, then managing battery drain is a much more important concern. That's because in order for your app to know where the phone is geographically, it requires that the phone's GPS receiver be turned on and receiving a signal. The longer the GPS receiver remains powered on, the more power will be drained from the battery.

Another common source of battery drain in an app is through the use of long-running background tasks. If you have an app that will run for long periods of time even while the user is in another app or not using the phone, that's another source of battery drain. An example of a common background task in mobile apps is *WIFI synchronization* of data, like is done with Spotify or the New York Times app. Music apps like Spotify rely on background tasks to synchronize data between the phone and a remote server. The amount of battery consumed by these background tasks is proportional to the amount of time they spend actively doing work. If a background task runs once an hour and only for 5 seconds, then in the grand scheme of things, it's not so bad. However, if you have a background tasks that executes every 5 minutes, and each time makes a call to a remote server to download data, then you will have a battery life problem.

Finally, the battery life impact of your app increases with the more visual animations and complex graphical processing your app performs. If you are building a racing gaming app, then you will be redrawing large parts of the phone screen very rapidly to convey the sense of motion to the user. Animating the screen is not a simple task and requires the phone's CPU to 'rev-up' and crunch the calculations necessary to know which pixels on the screen need to be re-drawn. Even if you aren't building a game, unbridled use of animations within your UI screens and employing fancy animated transitions between views of your app will likely increase the strain on the phone's battery.

Throughout the mobile app design process you will need to balance your desire to create an engaging user experience (which often uses animations) and the need to minimize the battery drain as a result of your app. Ensure that whenever you use an animation that it is serving a legitimate need within the app.

6.2

Data Plans Aren't Unlimited

Your app draining the phone's battery is a sin, but generally the worst-case outcome from doing so is inconveniencing your user. A far greater sin for your app to commit is chewing up the user's cellular data plan. That one could actually cost them money!

In the United States, most smartphone plans come with a monthly quota of data that a user is allowed to download/upload, ranging from 200MB – 2GB per month. Exceeding this quota can quickly add up to a lot of money as cellular providers charge per MB overage charges. Now, if you are building an app that is completely stand-alone and does not communicate over the Internet with a server or web site, then you have nothing to worry about. However, if you are building a photo sharing or video-streaming app, then you must be aware of the strain you will place on a user's data plan.

Media Type	Average Size
30 second video, 640x480px	4.5 MB
2 minute video, 640x480px	17 MB
iPhone 4s photo	2 MB

Figure 30: Typical file sizes for mobile media

Every time you display a photo, or allow a user to play a video, you are potentially introducing a surprisingly hefty download cost. If your app is going to display 20 pictures at a time in a Pinterest-like table layout, then in the worst case you might find yourself moving around 40MB of data every time the app displays this screen. If you plan for users to use your app say more than once a month, then it's not hard to see how much of an impact this will have on a data plan.

Luckily, there are some simple ways you can minimize the data plan footprint of your app. One tip to producing a data-sipping app is to never download the same piece of content more than once. The first time a person opens a photo, your app should contact whatever web address it's located at and download it. However, the second time the user opens up the picture, your app needs to be smart enough to know that it has already downloaded that file and that it should simply render its stored version rather than incurring the download cost again. This is called *caching* and it's a tried and true mechanism used to minimize download costs. You have already been a consumer to caching as all modern web browsers use *caches* to maintain local copies of data. The principle behind image caching in browsers is exactly how image caching on an app works.

Another easy way to minimize data transfer is by using multiple versions of photos, scaled to different sizes depending on where they are being displayed in your app. If you are displaying thumbnail sized pictures to a user (like a list of contacts), then it makes no sense to use high-quality pictures with 2MB file sizes. Instead, use a smaller, scaled down version of the same photo when you are displaying thumbnails. When the user taps to open one of these pictures, only then you should download a higher quality version of the photo.

Finally, another way to save data transfer costs is by designing your app to only show the user as much as they can reasonably be expected to act upon. If you want to show a list of pictures uploaded by other people with your app, you shouldn't display one giant list of photos. Instead, utilize the concept of *paging*, where only the first ten items are shown on the list; only when a user clicks a 'next' button or scrolls down to near the bottom of the list will your app retrieve the next set of data. Remember, these are mobile apps you are building. Do not expect people to ever make it to the bottom of a 100 item list.

6.3

Small Screens, Busy Hands, Poor Eyes, Fat Fingers

At the risk of pointing out the obvious, a mobile phone is not a laptop. There is no keyboard, the screens are generally pretty small, and people control them with their thumbs and forefingers. To compound matters, people are rarely ever just using their mobile phone; usually it is something they interact with as they move through parts of their day. More often than not, people are using their phone with only one hand and at a distance that of 2-3 feet from their eyes. All of these factors are things you do not need to worry about in the PC/Mac world. People use keyboards, mice and usually on screens that are at least 14 inches across. Not to mention users are stationary and glued to the task of operating the computer. Knowing this, designing a mobile app requires that you create user interfaces that are easily accessible by someone that is moving, distracted, or just plain clumsy with their hands. Thus, many of the traditional UI concepts you might be aware of in the web or desktop world are just not suitable in the mobile world. On the other hand, there are specific mobile layouts and gestures you should considering using when creating your app that are already tried and tested to be mobile-friendly and offer the same functionality.

Here are 3 well-known mobile UI patterns you app should look to leverage in your app:

Navigation Flow

The navigation flow pattern allows a user to move through your app while providing a breadcrumb to indicate where they are in the app. As a user taps and moves into a different screen, the breadcrumb (usually in the upper left corner) updates to indicate the previous screen. This design pattern is particularly helpful for moving a user through a wizard-like experience.

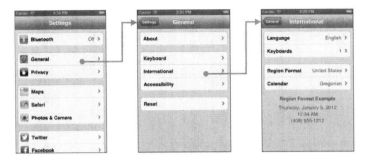

Figure 31: With a navigation flow, the title of the current screen and the back button work together to inform the user where they are in the app

List-to-Detail Views

Lists are a standard display metaphor in mobile apps. The commonly accepted way to display lists is to provide a picture and summary of the content within the list cells, and allow the user to drill into a 'detail' view by tapping a cell. Using the List-to-Detail metaphor along with the Navigation Flow concept, a user can easily move in and out cells in the table and not be disoriented as to their location within the app.

Figure 32: The iPhone Contacts app is a good example of a list-to-detail view in action

Tabs

Use tabs when you have multiple, independent experiences to provide to a user within your app. The tab bar exists along the bottom of the screen, and usually has 2-3 cells within it. Tab items are easily pressed with any finger, and are a simple, well-known metaphor for moving between different contexts within an app.

World Clock Tab   Stopwatch Tab   Timer Tab

Figure 33: The tabs of the iPhone Clock app clearly separate the different clock functions for the user

While at first glance a mobile app might resemble a website or desktop app, we assure you they represent an entirely new breed of software. Creating a great mobile app has as much to do with executing on a great idea as it does designing a user experience that is designed for mobile contexts.

As you move through your app development process, keep the lessons we have shared in mind. Take it from us, it's much easier and less costly to design with these constraints in mind than it is to fix them once you've released your app to the marketplace.

6.4

Don't Reinvent the UI Wheel

A mobile app is not the place to come up with a funky new UI style. While your desire to be unique may be strong, we assure you that introducing new user interface styles will only serve to confuse your users. When designing an app, you should leverage existing patterns and metaphors that users will already know and be familiar with. For instance people on the iPhone know that if they see an item in a list view, they can usually swipe once to the left across the cell to delete it. This is training and knowledge you should look to leverage; don't introduce new ways of doing tasks that users are already accustomed to performing on a smartphone. Using common design metaphors found in the mobile platform help make your app easier to use because users feel like they've used it before.

User Flow: Navigation vs. Overlays

Think of flow as the path a person cuts in your app as they move from screen to screen. People who use the iPhone will be fairly familiar with a navigation type of flow (where a breadcrumb/back button sits in the upper left corner of the title bar). A navigation flow is great for moving around the app while giving the user orientation as to where they are in the app. However, sometimes a navigational flow isn't the right choice for exposing all app functionality. Think of a login experience. This is usually a one-screen operation that a user may enter from any number of contexts in your app. In these cases, a overlay flow for the login page, where it slides up from the bottom of the screen conveys to the user that what they are looking at is a popup, or something very transitory and not part of the flow of the app.

Leverage Transitions

When your app moves from one screen to the next, how does that look? Realize that switching what the person is looking at instantaneously is very disorienting and is liable to confuse the user. If you are moving between screens, think about using animations to convey the motion between the two. People on iPhones are very used to the navigation metaphor of the slide transition as it tells them they are progressing into a 'detail' or 'sub' view. Users are also trained to know that a view that slides up from below and over top of the current screen is an overlay. The direction a new view appears on the screen and the speed at which it does so both serve to hold the user's hand as they interact with your app. Subtle use of animations is effective in keeping users engaged and oriented when using your app.

Use progress bars, don't leave your users hanging

It's ok if your app sometimes needs to make the user wait for some result to return from the server or for a calculation to finish. It's not ok to make a person wait and not give them any visual cue that the app is busy doing something. Progress bars are supremely important when it comes to mobile apps, as 3G (and even 4G/LTE) connections tend to get bogged down and even the most basic server calls can take time to execute. If you are building a photo-sharing app, understand that uploading a 500kb photo to a server can take up to 30 seconds and is liable to fail on a busy 3G connection. Putting up a progress bar with a spinning wheel and a description can go a long way to making a person ok with waiting. Progress bars are great places to distract users by displaying advertisements, useful tips, or even a funny joke. The worst thing you can do is have your app's UI lock up when it's busy performing a task and have the user tapping around trying to figure out why nothing is working.

Speed is relative

The speed of your app has less to do with the actual rate at which it completes a task and more to do with how long the user feels it took. For example, when a user presses a button, does the app respond immediately? Is there a lag between letting up the button and the screen reacting? Users have shockingly small attention spans and are more apt to double tap a button or control if there isn't an immediate response. You don't want to make your user wait for your app to respond, even if your app is busy processing an image or communicating with the server. You need to make sure that the user interface is either always accessible to input or, if not, there is a clear progress indicator which lets the user know what is going on. Use progress bars to pause the user when it is necessary, otherwise your app should leverage background tasks to complete remote operations that the user otherwise shouldn't be informed of.

An additional source of perceived speed in an app is the time it takes to open up after a user has tapped its icon. During the startup of your app, there is little you can do to speed it up. However, that shouldn't preclude you from using a splash screen or series of splash screens strung together as an animation to give the user an indication that the app is doing something and not 'hung'.

6.5

Designing Dani's List

Up till now we've only discussed Dani's List in abstract terms, now we'll actually start designing the app. Over the next few pages, we'll take what we've learned so far about Dani's List, including the user scenarios and the monetization opportunities, and start to sketch out the look and feel of the app. Through this exercise we'll not only end up with a good idea of how the app will work, but the exercise will force us to think through the app's functionality in greater detail and uncover potentially hidden issues.

Before we start designing the app, let's recall some of the hypothesis we made earlier on in the book about how people will use Dani's List:

- People will look to the app for inspiration or to generate ideas of things they can possibly occupy their time with over the period of a few days.

- Generally, people will use the app for browsing and planning while they are stationary and probably while bantering back and forth with one or more other people.

- People will need a simple way of selecting activities they want to do and placing them on their own personal to-do list.

- Users will typically have a few (probably less than three) constraints they will want to use when finding new things to do. These constraints can include the distance from their current location, type of activity (something to eat vs. something to do), amount they want to spend, current time of day, current weather and desire to be outdoors or indoors.

- People will come back to their own personal list of activities periodically through the day. In these cases, they'll likely be crossing things off that they've done, looking for the next thing to do, or digging in to get more details (like the address, contact, photo) of the next activity they are heading towards. In these situations, people can expect to be moving about and

126

not completely stationary.

- Some people, upon completing an activity they liked, will want to share that experience with their friends who might also one day be in the area. Most likely they'll want to share this via Facebook or Twitter.

Given these statements, we generalize that a user opening the app will either be looking to manage/view their own personal 'what-do-list' of activities or to discover new activities around them to add to their list. We imagine that users will want to switch between viewing their personal what-to-do list and discovering new activities quite frequently while in the app. To make it easy for a user to switch between these two contexts, we'll use what is called a *Segmented Control* to allow users to flip between the two views. A Segmented Control looks like two buttons joined together at the sides. When a user taps one of buttons in a segmented control, it becomes selected and appears to remain 'pressed'. If the user selects the other button it will become 'pressed' and the other button will appear 'unpressed'. We'll use the segmented control to let users move between viewing their personal what-to-do list of activities and discovering other activities nearby that they can add to their list.

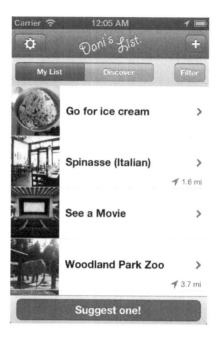

Figure 34: A Segmented Control allows users to switch between viewing their personal list ('My List'), and activities created by others ('Discover')

Managing a User's What-to-Do List of Activities

In the case of a user viewing their own what-to-do list of activities, we can model this to look and feel like a to-do list. Beyond being a well-known metaphor to most people, the to-do list allows us to tap into the psychological feeling of achievement that comes from 'crossing' things off. We can create a powerful emotional connection with users by making it very easy to 'cross off' items on the list, and then give them visual cues of the item being crossed-off the list to cultivate the feeling of accomplishment. We can do this in a couple of different ways: we can animate an actual line being drawn across the item to show it being 'crossing-off', or just animate the removal of the item of the list.

As for the actual items on their list, we need to design them to convey just enough information so the user is able to recall what it is without cluttering the screen. Remember that it's likely that users will visit this part of the app throughout the day, and that they will likely not be sitting down or still when doing so. Thus, we need to make sure each item is tall enough so that a user can see it while holding their phone at a distance. However, since we want to show people a 'list' of their activities, we can't make each item too tall otherwise the list metaphor might be lost. With that in mind, we'll use the *List-Detail UI* metaphor when creating this view. A user will be displayed a list of their personal activities, with each item containing just a picture and description of the activity. The user can then tap any item to move into a detail view of the particular activity.

For each item in their what-to-do list of activities, we can make it easy for a user to cross-off any activity as being complete by using the swipe gesture. When a user swipes left across any item on their activity list, we will display the ability for the user to mark the item being 'done' and remove it. The swipe across a list item is a commonly used metaphor on iOS, and is one most users would already be trained to expect when working with list views. Thus, by adapting this well-known pattern for managing items on list, we've avoided having to train users how to interact with our app and made the experience that much more straightforward.

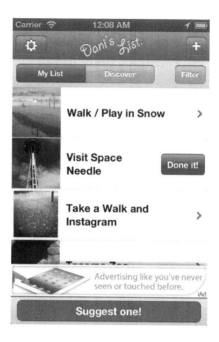

Figure 35: A swipe across the table cell reveals a 'Done it!' button

When a user taps a particular item on their list, they will move into the detail view for that particular activity. It's in this view that a user will be able to see all the details of the activity that includes: name of activity, category, weather, time of day, price range and map. We'll use the standard iOS navigation pattern to show a 'back' button in the upper left corner that will give users a visual cue that they are in a detail view. An important aspect of the List-Detail metaphor is to ensure that the transition between the list view and the detail view is animated so that the detail screen slides in from the right. This animation gives the user the feeling that they are drilling-into the list and is consistent with how users interact with lists in iOS.

Within the detail view of an activity, a user has the ability to view all the properties of the activity by scrolling up and down the view. On the title bar we will display the 'back' button in the upper left, the name of the activity in the center, and an 'edit' button in the upper right. When a user presses the 'edit' button it allows them to edit any property of the activity. Again, we can make it visually clear to the user that they are now in an edit mode by overlaying a view of the activity that allows the user to modify any field of the activity. When this overlay is displayed, instead of showing a 'back' and 'edit' button, we will show a 'cancel' and 'done' button.

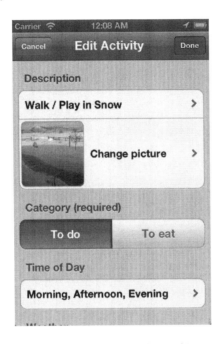

Figure 36: The Edit overlay, notice the 'Done' button in the upper right corner

Unlike the transition between the list and detail views that had the detail view slide in from the right, when a user presses the 'edit' button the overlay will slide overtop the detail view from the bottom. This transition will give the user a visual indication that they are 'stationary' in that they have not moved into another activity. When the user presses either the 'done' or 'cancel' buttons, the overlay will disappear by sliding down and revealing the details of the updated activity.

Creating a New Activity

In Dani's List, people can add activities to their list in two ways: they can add an activity that has already been created by someone else through the 'Discover' list, or they can create their own activity from scratch.

In the latter case, a user will typically have an idea of something they want to do and will need a simple way to enter this item into Dani's List. A brainstorm can hit a user at any time, so we need to make the user experience of creating an activity as simple as possible without requiring the user to fill out lots of input fields just to add a new activity. Since a user can edit an activity at any time through the detail view, we don't want the creation experience to have a bunch of fields that require the user to input information into before they can save an activity. So, if a user is walking down the street and has an idea for something to do that is nearby, we'll require that they only provide a description and category (i.e. 'something to eat' vs. 'something to do') for the activity before they can save it. Creating a new activity from scratch is a common task that should be accessible to the user when viewing both their own list and a list of nearby activities, so we'll put a '+' button on the right side of the title bar for both of these views.

Figure 37: The '+' allows a user to add a new activity to their list from both the 'My List' and 'Discover' list

When a user taps the '+' button, we will transition to a create activity view. We'll use an overlay slide transition from the bottom to signify to the user that they are performing an action that is independent from the list view. The create activity view will be similar in appearance to the detail view of an activity, except no fields will be populated. To make it easy for someone to quickly create a new activity, the 'description' and 'category' options are displayed at the top. The user can easily type in the description and select the appropriate category using a switch control and save it. Below these two fields are additional pieces of data a user can attach to the activity, like a photo, budget, rating, location, weather and expiry date of the activity. We'll use the title bar to display a 'cancel' button on the left, and a 'done' button on the right to let the user exit the view by either saving or abandoning the activity they are creating.

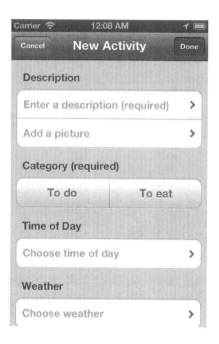

Figure 38: User's create a new activity by filling out this view which is overlaid over the main view of the app

To make it easy for a user to populate all of these fields, we will use pre-populated lists of acceptable values that a user can choose from for each field. When a user taps a field, we transition into another view that shows all the values that a user can choose for that field. Since the user is drilling into a particular field, we use a slide transition to display a new view with a list of acceptable values for the user to choose from. Just like sliding into a detail view of an activity, when a user enters the value selection view for a field we will display a 'back' button on the left side of the title bar to let them move back into the main creation view. Since most fields can have more than one value, we mark each value selected with a checkmark.

Figure 39: Users can select values for a new activity by tapping one or more values, selected values are check marked

When a user has finished selecting the values for a particular field, they will press the 'back' button to slide back into the create activity view. The field that they added values to will now show the values they selected. At any point the user can tap the field again and they will move back into the value selection screen with all values selected marked with a checkbox.

Discovering New Activities

One of the cool ideas behind Dani's List is to let a user view activities added by other people via the 'Discover' list. In this view, a user will be in an exploratory mode looking for interesting things that they may want to add to their own list. The key pieces of information that they will likely want to see about other people's activities are: the description, a picture and a relative distance from their location. Again, we'll use a simple List-Detail metaphor to show users a short summary of an activity in a list view, and then more details about each activity in a separate detail view.

Figure 40: Activities in a list are displayed with an image, description and relative distance

Selecting any activity will transition into a detail view that is the same as the detail views of the activities on the user's personal to-do list. For each item on this list view, a user will be able to swipe across to expose the options of 'add to my list' which, when clicked, will add the activity to their own what-to-do list.

Another important function for a user viewing a list of activities is the ability for them to filter what they see based on their own preferences for what they'd like to do. We'll need to have a way a user can filter the list of activities to show only those that match their tastes. We'll add a 'filter' button to the top of the list that, when tapped, will move into a filter screen. When a user presses 'filter', a filter view will slide in as an overlay of the list view from the bottom.

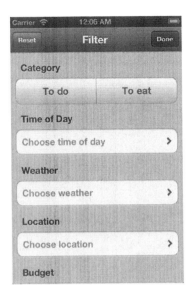

Figure 41: Users can filter the list of activities using the same experience used to create an activity; no filters (left) and filters selected (right)

The filter view is meant to make it easy for users who are moving about to specify their own preferences for what they'd like to find. Users can filter activities by selecting values for each of the fields of an activity that they are interested in. This view looks similar to the creation and detail views of an activity, with the same controls and values used to create the filter condition. By using the same layout for all three of these contexts, we teach the user to recognize any of those screens as being centered on activities.

Furthermore, we'll save time and effort when it comes to development by using a single visual metaphor for the create, edit, view and filter actions on an activity. When a user is done creating their filter preferences, they'll be able to press 'done' on the right side of the tool bar, which will slide down the filter screen to show the activity list again. The activity list will then be whittled down to only show activities that match the filter. We can give users a visual cue that they are looking at a filtered list of activities by highlighting the 'filter' button whenever a filter has been defined.

Figure 42: The now orange 'Filtered' button indicates to the user the current list they are viewing is a filtered list

7

Managing App Development

Apps don't build themselves, even if you already have someone to design it and another to code it. and leads them to play a symphony, Like a conductor leading an orchestra to produce a harmonious symphony, you need to bring together your designers, engineers and others so that their work culminates in the creation of your app. If this is the first time you've managed a software project, then let me remind you of one of the most important commandments of app development: your timeline will slip.

Figure 43: Be ready for your schedule to change as your app is developed

Building software is not like building a house, a car, or any other manufactured item. For one, software has no physical manifestation. You can't go out to the production line and see for yourself how it looks and how it is coming along. A mobile app under development exists only within the engineer's head and, at best, as a rudimentary prototype on a phone. The intangible nature of what you are building makes it difficult for project managers to keep an accurate pulse of their project, as they are largely beholden to what their engineers tell them. Generally, with software development projects, you can expect the first 1-2 months of development to be completely invisible to you with very little that can be demonstrated in its final form.

Furthermore, Murphy's Law is as much a truth in software development as is Moore's Law. It is impossible to build bug free software and you should expect that during the development process you will encounter many bugs, some of them minor and others much more major. Your goal as a project manager is to limit the impact to the schedule these bugs have by instituting enough process to minimize the number of major destabilizing bugs from cropping up. Major bugs are those that expose a critical flaw in your design and require substantial redesign and coding to fix.

140

7.1

The Tragedy of Longhorn

The good news is that nobody has figured out how to build software on time and on budget. Not even giants like Microsoft. If you remember the much-maligned Windows Vista, it was the product of a colossal failure in project management. In 2001, after shipping Windows XP, Microsoft set out to revolutionize its flagship operating system with a new version named 'Longhorn' slated for release in 2003. Longhorn was hugely ambitious, with many new technologies planned for introduction in one single release. However, the development process at Microsoft was haphazard and lacking any central control and guidance. The result was that each engineering team set out to build their little corner of Longhorn, but nobody was ensuring all the pieces fit together right and that they all worked as one.

We'll let Bobby (who's Bobby? one of the co-authors of this book!) take over and tell the rest of the Longhorn story:

I joined Microsoft as an intern in 2004 and I remember installing an early build of Longhorn hoping to see how the new operating system looked and worked. After installing Longhorn, I booted it up, logged in and clicked on the 'Start' button. Nothing seemed to happen. I clicked 'Start' again and the machine blue-screened and crashed. I was just an intern, but even then I was puzzled at how something as vital as Windows and so far along in development in Longhorn could be that broken. I wasn't alone. A few weeks later, Jim Allchin, the Senior Vice President who oversaw all development of Windows, came to the conclusion that the project couldn't be salvaged and he ordered a complete reset of the Longhorn project. All work done until then was thrown out, and the project began again in 2004 and was eventually released in a somewhat incomplete state as Windows Vista in 2006.

Longhorn failed, just like many other software projects do, because there was no leadership to herd the engineers and ensure everybody was marching in the same direction. The engineers were essentially left to their own devices, which meant that while they diligently worked on their features, they operated without knowledge of and concern for how all the pieces fit together.

Another lesson from Longhorn was the danger in doing too much in a single release. With Longhorn, Microsoft wanted to rebuild Windows almost from the ground up all at once. Software development requires engineers to take dependencies on other engineers' code, and if the code they are dependent on continues to change underneath them then that is liable to break their code. In Longhorn, so many pieces were constantly changing and there were so many bugs in the resulting changes that engineers couldn't do their work because what they relied on was broken. Longhorn taught Microsoft, and should teach you, that it's much better to have shorter schedules with minimal amounts of functionality than to have a long release schedule with a ton of changes crammed in it.

Finally, another failure of the Longhorn project was performance and reliability not being given the proper attention during the design and planning phases of the project. Management failed to define both the performance goals that every component had to meet, but it also didn't ensure that performance testing was done at an early enough point in the project that issues could be identified and fixed. When I installed Longhorn on that fateful day in 2004, it took 5 minutes for the machine to boot up!

While Longhorn was a multi-billion dollar project with thousands of people working on it, its lessons are just as applicable to your mobile app project. The same things that sunk Longhorn - poor management, scope creep and performance - are just as likely to happen to your project. You are the project manager for your app, and even though you might not know how to code, you need to be the conductor of your orchestra. Unless you find engineers who understand your vision completely, you cannot hope to put your project on cruise control and have it build itself. If you don't ensure things are progressing on schedule, and that the engineers are making the right decisions, nobody will.

7.2

The Mobile App Development Process

Managing a software project is tough. If you are in charge of the effort, you not only need to be well-versed enough in the technology to know what your engineers are saying to you, but you also need the intuition and decisiveness to set the direction for your team.

Luckily for you the software renaissance of recent years has brought with it new methodologies for managing software projects that you can use to keep your project on track. However, you need to remember that these are best practices and adopting a methodology as religion can do as much damage to your development as not having any methodology at all. Every project is different, and you will need to be able to take the best parts of each framework and apply it as needed.

In this chapter, we will outline the methodology we use when developing mobile apps for ourselves and for our clients. You should look to this methodology as a how-to guide to managing your project and not a rigid set of rules to follow. The truth of building software is that each project is different and depending who you are working with and what your timeline is, you will need to manage your project according to your own intuition rather than to the letter of a methodology.

The methodology we use for building an app can be described with these 5 milestones:

1. Design & Planning
2. Development & Test
3. Release
4. Gather Feedback
5. Go back to 1 and repeat

You shouldn't view these milestones as a linear set of steps; they are more like a cycle. Each cycle is called a *release* and ends with a finished product being made available on an app marketplace. While we all want to release an amazing app on the first go, the reality is that your first release probably won't be very good. You need to assume this going in and aim to develop your app over a series of releases. The commandment that you need to follow here is "release early and often". The more you are able to iterate and get your app in the hands of your users, the more feedback you'll get to develop it further and improve it. In our experience, it usually takes 3-4 iterations of this process before we've built an app that we can truly say is 'finished'.

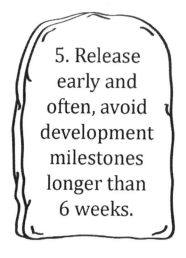

Figure 44: Quick releases let you test and develop your app based on user feedback

Concerning Beta Releases

Going back to the commandments we introduced at the start of the book, when it comes to managing the app development process you need to focus on doing less, releasing quickly, getting feedback and then doing it all over again. Your first release will generally take the longest to complete since you are starting from nothing. Do not expect your app to be 'done' after one release; it takes much iteration before you will reach a point where you'll believe it's done. These intermediary releases of an unfinished product are commonly referred to as *beta* releases.

Typically with a team of 2 engineers, a simple social networking app (like Bahndr on the iPhone) usually takes 2-3 months before the first beta version is released to the app store. The first beta isn't very polished, and we are often hesitant to show it to too many people because it is still buggy and not functionally complete. However, the first beta demonstrates the essence of the app, even if it's in a rough and unpolished form. By demonstrating a basic scenario and watching how other people use and react to it we can validate the assumptions we've made about why people would want to use the app and if they would come back to using it. Far from being a public release, the first release of our apps are usually private and restricted to a few handpicked people who we work with personally to see how they use the app.

In the case of Dani's List, we consider the first beta release of the app to include the core functionality of the app: creating activities, completing them and finding new ones. While our plans for Dani's List include more functionality than that, for the first beta release of the app we sacrifice breadth of functionality for validation of the concept.

When your app is in beta your focus shouldn't be on monetization, but rather you should focus on validating the essence of the app. For our beta release of Dani's List, we've chosen to skip functionality such as the social media sharing and much of the freemium functionality. Instead, we focused on building the core user experience of the app in the first release of Dani's List. From here, we can validate our own hypothesis of how we think people will use the app and base our next release off of what we learn from the beta.

You shouldn't expect, neither should you attempt, your app to go viral during its early beta releases. The truth of betas is that they are very rough, buggy, and generally don't serve to make a great first impression to a user who doesn't know it's a beta release. Thus, even before you release you first beta, you should start selecting amongst your friends, colleagues and classmates those who you think will want to use your beta.

Step 1: Design & Planning

The one phase that most software projects get wrong is the first:

Design & Planning. In most projects, and especially with startups, there is a huge rush to jump into development at the expense of clearly articulating the goals of the release. Don't do this, no matter how well you think the vision is understood by you and your team. Having it codified in paper will go a long way to keeping development on track. At the end of the Design & Planning phase you should have:

1. A mock-up or wireframe document illustrating every screen of your app with all colors, logos, and other design assets.
2. A prioritized scenario document outlining all of the customer use cases your release aims to enable.
3. A prioritized functional specification document which outlines in detail how your app will look, the desired behavior of the app, and the requirements for each piece of functionality.
4. A development schedule that outlines the target dates for scenarios to be completed, testing goals and desired release dates.

Mock-ups & Wireframes

One of the first things you should do when starting down the road of building a mobile app is to create a mock-up / wire-frame drawing of your app. A mock-up is essentially a non-functional prototype of your app designed to illustrate the look and feel of your app. Mock-ups are meant to give a visual impression to the reader of what your app will look like, but also how users will move through the various screens of your app. A wireframe is very much like a mockup, however wireframes tend to be black and white and focus more on the overall user flow of in the app.

Mock-ups are extremely useful in the early stages of your app development to help communicate your idea to others and to test the concepts behind it. If you plan on financing your app development from outside investors, then having a detailed mock-up of your app will go a long way to communicating your vision to potential investors.

Furthermore, once you are ready to proceed with app

development, a mock up allows your graphic designer to visually ascertain your app and helps her move forward creating the necessary graphics and logos your app will need. For developers, a good mockup will allow them to get a better idea of how the app will work and how users will move through the different views of the app. A good mockup will uncover issues with both user flow and technical complexity, hopefully saving you time that might have been used to fix them later on in development.

Creating a mockup isn't very difficult or time consuming. As we mentioned earlier on in this book, you can either use dedicated mockup tools, like Balsamiq, or general-purpose image editing software like Photoshop. The easiest way to create a mockup for your app is to use Microsoft PowerPoint or Apple's Keynote software. You can purchase mockup templates online which contain all major UI components and controls for iPhone, Android and Windows Phone platforms. With these, you simply copy and paste together a mockup or wireframe for your app right inside PowerPoint.

Unlike the scenario and functional specification documents, you should create a mockup very early in your app development cycle. Before you have financing, before you find an engineer, before you've found a designer, you need to have a mockup!

A great mockup is easy to create and gives you a tangible asset that you can use to communicate your app concept to investors, developers, designers and potential customers.

Step 1: Design & Planning

Wireframes: *One of the first things you should do when starting down the road of building a mobile app is creating a mock-up / wire-frame of your app. A mock-up is essentially a non-functional prototype of your app designed to illustrate the look and feel of your app. Here are a few of the original screen mockups we created for Dani's List using Apple Keynote and a wireframing tool called Keynotopia. There are many tools available to make wireframing and prototyping easy for anyone; more examples are listed below.*

Tool	Description	Price (est.)
Keynotopia	Apple Keynote and Microsoft PowerPoint UI templates. Good for iOS and Android apps.	$50 - $100
Windows8Templates	Microsoft PowerPoint UI templates. Good for Windows 8 and Windows Phone 8 apps. Mockups can be made clickable on a Windows 8 device.	$50 - $100
Balsamiq	Web-based design tool that mimics low-fidelity hand drawn sketching of app wireframes.	$80
Proto.io	Web-based UI prototyping tool with support for full feature animations and clickable actions.	$25 - $50 / month
Photoshop	Profession design software by Adobe that allows you to create realistic mockups with full-color rendering, and highly-detailed screen design.	$600

Figure 45: Mockups and wireframes let you simulate how your app will look and behave

Scenario Documents

In the Design & Planning phase, you first need to agree within your team on what it is that you are looking to achieve with this release. One way of specifying the goals of the release is to list a set of functionality you'd like to be included in it. While this is useful, you shouldn't look at your release as being a sum of the functionality within it. A better way to outline the goals of a release is to do so from a customer's perspective. Instead of listing what features are in the release, you outline the scenarios that you'd like the customer to be able to perform with the release. The benefit of the customer scenario oriented approach is that you are avoiding the common pitfall of shipping a product that has a lot of independent functionality that doesn't fit together in one coherent story.

Your Design & Planning milestone should start with drafting a prioritized list of scenarios into a 'Scenario Document'. A scenario document serves as the codification of the goals of your release. A good scenario document outlines important details about the people who will be using it, the contexts they will be operating in and the specific things they'd like to accomplish. A scenario document shouldn't refer to specific pieces of functionality or to the layout of your app; it is but a description of needs and goals of a user in a particular setting. Your scenario document serves as the foundation for defining requirements and designing functionality for your release.

The reality of software development is you will not be able to achieve all of your scenarios with your current release. Problems happen, bugs crop up, and eventually you'll need to make tough decisions as to which scenarios you keep and which ones you 'cut' or 'punt' to the next release. To prepare you for this eventuality, your list of scenarios needs to also include a relative prioritization of the importance of each.

A Primer on Prioritization

If this is your first time through the software development loop, get ready to hear the term 'prioritization' thrown at you endlessly. Prioritization is the process of attaching a value to a task/feature/scenario and then ordering what gets done first by those with the highest priority attached to it.

When you are planning your release, you will use prioritization to attach value to the scenarios you are looking to enable with the release. You will use these priorities to schedule when specific items are developed and help you fix bugs that emerge during development.

A common nomenclature for prioritization is the simple 3-step priority scale that is used at Microsoft:

- **Priority 0 (P0)**

P0s represent the highest priority items to be completed. A P0 is defined as something so critical to the release of the product that you would hold the release to include/fix it. By definition, there should be no outstanding P0 tasks at the end of the release, otherwise it wasn't a real P0.

- **Priority 1 (P1)**

P1s are high priority items, but they aren't necessarily things you would hold up a release for. Releasing a product with outstanding P1 bugs is painful, because a P1 is still a major bug that someone might notice, yet it is one you are willing to live with. An example of a P1 bug would be your app not being able to install on an older iPhone. While this is might be a major bug, it usually isn't enough to warrant you holding up the entire release of your product to fix.

- **Priority 2 (P2)**

P2 is the 'other' bucket where bugs end up when they aren't important enough to be considered P1s. You should view P2 items as things that are "nice to have," rather than "must have." P2 items can be anything from changes in color schemes to re-designing UI flow. A sad reality of app development is that there are usually so many P0s and P1s that you might not ever get around to something marked as a P2. Typically the first few beta releases of an app are so chock-full of bugs or missing functionality that P2 bugs only ever get fixed in the final release once the app has stabilized.

Once you have prioritized your list of scenarios, you then have a reasonable plan of action for your release. The scenarios you've marked as being P0 are showstoppers, so you will not release without those scenarios working. Use the priorities you place on the scenarios for your release to drive how you make decisions regarding bugs and other changes that will come up during the development milestone.

Scenario Document: *A good scenario document outlines important details about the people who will be using it, the contexts they will be operating in and the specific things they'd like to accomplish. List key user scenarios for your app, then assign a priority level to each. The good thing is you've already started thinking about scenarios in the brainstorming phase...right?*

#	Description	Priority P0 = show stopping P1 = not release critical P2 = everything else
Ex.	*Dani's List User Scenario: Users will typically have a few (probably less than 3) constraints they will want to use when finding new things to do.*	*P0*
1		
2		
3		
4		
5		
6		
7		

Figure 46: Scenario documents are important to understanding what your customer's intend to do with your app

Functional Specifications

If a scenario document outlines what users will be able to accomplish in your release, then a *Functional Specification* outlines how they will use your app to accomplish their goals. A functional specification serves as blueprint for your developers, testers and anyone else involved in the project as to how your app will look and behave. If you already have mockups or designs for how your app will look, then this is a good place to start building a functional specification.

A starting point for building a functional specification is to map each scenario outlined in your scenario document and map it to a sequence of steps and actions that the user will need to perform in your app. Once you've mapped out a few scenarios, you should start to get a good idea of the features you will need to build, along with the various UI elements that will need to support the scenarios. While you could build your functional specification by mapping every scenario to its constituent steps in the app, you will find yourself mired in copying entire sections of steps and suffering to keep requirements consistent between them.

A better way to approach functional specification of an app is to take a UI-centered approach to outlining the details of your app. In this approach, you need to specify both the navigation flow between one view and the next, along with details on how each view looks and behaves. A simple way to capture the navigation flow is to use a flow diagram to show the movement of a user between the views of your app for each scenario.

A flow diagram is a series of steps, connected by directional arrows that illustrate a user's progression through your app to complete a task. At each step is the name of one of the UI views that make up your app or decision point taken by the user within a view. You can use the arrows between each view to specify details on how transitions and animations between each screen should behave.

Once you have outlined the various navigation flows in your app, you can take each UI view and specify their behavior. With each view, you should break down the look and feel of each UI component, along with what action is to happen when users interact with them. You'll find that many of the UI views in your app will be reused depending on what the user is attempting to do, so make sure when you specify them to take all of these scenarios into account.

Here are a few tips to writing good functional specifications:

- Speak in an active voice and avoid ambiguity in your prose. Avoid verbs like 'should' and 'may', and instead use 'must', 'will'.
- Remember to think about performance and scale considerations. Make sure to outline clearly in your specification any requirements on the maximum amount of time for a user to wait, along with the number of users the app will need to support.
- Think of different ways people can use your app that might not be obvious or mainstream cases and make sure your specification handles the behavior of your app in those circumstances.
- Prioritize functionality in your specification using the priorities of the scenarios they are linked to as a guide.
- Your specification should not delve into technical jargon, as that's a sign you are over-detailing. You are creating a blueprint; leave it to your developers to fill in the details.
- Remember to outline how your app should react to *offline*\ scenarios with no Internet connection and on slow 3G networks.
- Don't write in a vacuum. Make sure to involve your developers and testers throughout the specification process.

A functional specification is a living document, and you shouldn't expect it to be 'finished' before moving into development. The functional specification is both a blueprint for what to build and documentation for what actually gets built. As you move through development and testing, always go back to the specification as the ultimate source of truth for how things should look and behave. A functional specification is meant to change and should always reflect the current state of the app, even if that means re-writing portions of the specification.

Functional Specification: *If a scenario document outlines what users will be able to accomplish in your release, then a 'Functional Specification' outlines how they will use your app to accomplish their goals. A functional specification serves as blue print for your developers, testers and anyone else involved in the project as to how your app will look and behave. Follow this example of a P0 user scenario from Dani's List and map out the movement of a user between the views of your app for each scenario. Don't forget to address 'corner-cases', such as 'no-connection' scenarios.*

#	Dani's List User Scenario	Priority
Ex.	Users will typically have a few (probably less than 3) constraints they will want to use when finding new things to do. These constraints can include: • **Distance from their current location** • Type of activity (something to eat vs. something to do) • Amount they want to spend • Current time of day • Current weather • Desire to be outdoors or indoors	P0

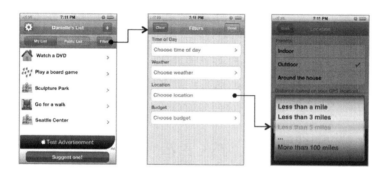

Figure 47: Start your specification by mapping your user scenarios to your mockups

154

Flow Diagram: *The user wants to filter their list of activities by a distance of 5 miles from their current location.*

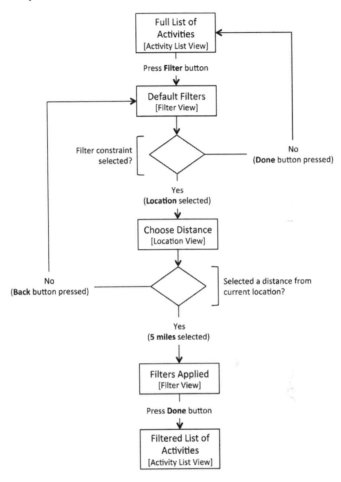

Figure 48: You can translate the user flow presented on the previous page into a flow chart like this to include as part of your Functional Specification

Step 2a: Development

This is where the rubber meets the road, when things actually get built. Development is when your engineers take the mockups, scenario document and functional specification and begin bringing it to life. This by far the most critical time for your release, and you need to be prepared for any number of issues to crop up.

When planning your release, you want to ensure that you keep your development milestones as short as possible. While keeping the development milestone short means cutting functionality and scaling back your ambitions, it will limit the financial drain on your resources and ultimately help you keep your business afloat. You want your development milestones to be more like three- to four-week sprints, rather than one- to two-month slogs. By keeping too long of a development milestone you not only suffer the cost of paying for engineering time, but also you are limiting the amount of work that might need to be discarded. The crux of the mobile app development process is iteration based on user feedback. If you rush headlong into a two-month development milestone to build out an entire set of features for your app, you risk the chance that you will need to go back and either redesign, or potentially rip out the work that was done during that time. You cannot afford your developers to spend time building things that need to be re-done or pulled out, so ensure your release schedule only contains the bare amount of work needed to achieve your scenario goals.

When you are building from scratch, you can expect your first development milestone to be the longest. It will take time for your engineering team to lay down the necessary foundations for getting your app to work and much of what they will be doing will be deep in the foundations of the app, things that you won't be able to see. Furthermore, it is likely that for first few weeks of development, you won't have anything to see and test. Again, you shouldn't be concerned about your progress in these cases. The truth of software development is that things tend to come together very quickly once the foundations of an application have been built.

Step 2b: Testing

We cannot emphasize enough the importance of testing your app while it's in development! Programming is an error-prone endeavor. Even the most talented of developers will introduce bugs into the app. While your developers are focused day-to-day on writing code, you need to make sure that you and other people are installing what they build and verifying that all of the functionality works according to spec.

Testing is as much an art as is writing code. The mindset you need to take when testing your app is, "What are the various ways I can break it?" Don't just assume that since your app works fine along the major use cases (what we like to call the 'happy path') that it contains no bugs. Trust us, it does. When testing, you need to explore all different combinations of potential user actions and ensure that the app continues to function.

It's helpful to create a list of test cases, known as a *Test Plan*, that you want to verify work on the app prior to releasing it. You can then use these list of test cases to determine whether or not you are ready to ship. The test cases you put on your Test Plans should derive themselves from the scenarios you intend to light up with the release. Furthermore, you should prioritize each test case to reflect the priority of the scenario they are associated with. You won't always have enough time to run through an entire gamut of tests, but by prioritizing them you will make sure the tests you do run test the most important functionality of the app.

Testing Intermediary Builds

Once your developers have completed the basic foundation of your app, you can begin testing it on your phone. You don't have to wait until the release to the App Store in order to test an app under development; all of the major platforms provide the ability to distribute development builds.

A particularly useful tool for distributing and managing test builds of your app under development is Test Flight (http://www.testflightapp.com). This free portal provides a single management point for you to upload builds, distribute them to specified test users, and then obtain feedback and communicate with them. If you are building an iPhone app, you will need to sign the build produced by your engineers with an Ad-Hoc Provisioning Profile obtained from the Apple Developer web site. The Ad-Hoc

Provisioning Profile allows you to distribute your app to up to 99 different phones outside of the app store through services like Test Flight.

Figure 49: TestFlight is a simple and free way to test your app while it's in development

Unit Testing

Developers hate testing. They loathe it! You can't blame them either. They like to build things, not break them. However, just because developers do not like testing doesn't mean you should let them off without any test burden. You want to create a quality app that people want to use, and you need to make sure quality is as important to the developer as shipping on time.

One popular way to both ensure and emphasize quality to your developers is by adopting the use of *Unit Tests*. A unit test is a small piece of code, written by a developer, designed to test a basic scenario for whatever component a developer might be working on. Thus, every time a developer adds a new feature, they also create a few unit tests to verify the basic scenarios of that feature work. Unit tests are usually built within a unit testing framework, and they can be run on demand at any time.

The benefit of unit testing is twofold: you ensure the quality of your product by having automated tests covering each piece of functionality, and you emphasize a quality-first mindset by requiring that developers ensure all unit tests pass before checking in their code for a new feature.

If you adopt unit testing from the get go, you will greatly simplify the later development and release stages of the app. Unit tests provide a very simple and quick way for anybody to verify that the app functions at a basic level. The unit testing framework you use to build and manage unit tests will depend on the mobile platform you are building on and the preference of your developers. Leave the choice of framework up to them, but make sure that everyone buys into the unit testing mindset.

Things to remember when testing a mobile app

Mobile apps by their very nature require you to test your apps in a variety of scenarios and conditions that might not be obvious at first glance, here are a few:

- **Strength of the cellular signal**

Your developers are likely to test your app only while their phones are connected to a Wi-Fi connection, which are much faster and more reliable than any cellular connection. The quality of a cellular signal is a function of geographic location, the time of day, and any physical obstructions that might be around you. Make sure you are testing all of your scenarios while connected to a regular cellular network and during the peak times when the bandwidth might be congested. By testing on 3G, you will be able to see how your app reacts to poor connection environments and expose many bugs which would go unseen on a Wi-Fi connection.

- **Screen Orientation**

Smartphones and tablets can usually be held in two positions: landscape and portrait. Landscape mode is when the user holds the phone on its side with the longest sides of the phone at the top and bottom. Portrait is when the user holds the phone normally with the longest sides at the left and right. When you move from one mode to the other, the mobile operating system will send a signal to your app informing it to adjust its screen layout to the new orientation. Often, developers overlook the adjustments that need to be made to the screen layout of the app when it moves into Landscape mode or vice versa. Test all of your main scenarios in both orientations; you are likely to find numerous bugs because of it.

- **Offline Behavior**

People living in New York are liable to go underground into the subways with your app open. There is no cellular signal in most subways - how will your app behave? If you are creating a social networking app that depends on an internet connection to perform most of its functionality, you need to ensure that when your phone loses its cellular connection, the app is smart enough to know this and display an error message to the user or operate in some predefined 'offline' mode.

Step 2: Development

Test Plan: *Create a list of test cases, known as a Test Plan that you want to verify work on the app prior to releasing it. The test cases you put on your Test Plans should derive themselves from the scenarios you intend to light up with the release. Furthermore, you should prioritize each test case to reflect the priority of the scenario they are associated with.*

#	Test Case	Pre-Requisites	Expected Result	Pri.
Ex.	A user wants to find new activities in Dani's List based on the following 3 filter constraints: • Location = Distance within 5 miles of current location • Time-of-day = Afternoon or Evening • Budget = Free	• At least 2 activities in the Public List that meet this criteria • At least 4 activities in the Public List that do not meet this criteria	Of the 6 activities in the list, only the 2 that meet the filtered criteria remain after the filters have been applied	P0
1				
2				
3				
4				
5				
6				
7				

Figure 50: Create test plans to ensure your app is free of major bugs before release

Step 3: Release

It's the moment you been waiting for, when all the toil, sweat and tears bear fruit and you experience the sweet thrill of releasing your app. While that sounds fun in a book, in reality, releasing your app isn't so much like pushing a button and launching a missile as it is dropping a rock into water and watching the waves ripple outwards. The release process deals with the steps you'll take to move from the Development & Test phase to pushing your app up to the app marketplace for the world to enjoy.

You'll know you are ready to release your app when you are able to demonstrate all of your P0 scenarios for the release with no outstanding P0 issues. If you hold true to the concepts of prioritization, then this would be the absolute minimum threshold you would need to meet before you can release your app. Now every situation is different, and it's really up to you to decide how much work you want to put in to fix or include P1/P2 issues prior to releasing your app. In general, you want to avoid the trap of thinking, "Let's fix one more thing," or, "Let's just include this one small feature". The truth is, you'll find yourself endlessly grasping for perfection and investing time to fix things that might not even be noticed by users. The success of your app isn't predicated on achieving perfection; most of the time, 'good enough' is all you need.

Throughout the entire development process, your highest priority must be to get the app into the hands of your customer. The longer you spend fixing low priority bugs or adding minor functionality, the more time you take away from getting people to use the product and for you to understand how to make it better. Quite often, the first version of the app you release will look nothing like the second version, and all the work you put into fixing a bug would have been wasted. The mantra of "release often, and iterate" requires you to operate knowing that what you release in this version could be completely different than what comes in the next. Thus, to minimize wasted effort and time, hold yourself to a very strict bar of what priority items you will complete in a release and what things will have to wait for the next one.

Release Checklist

Apps don't live in a vacuum, and launching one on an app store requires prep work on your part. If you are launching your first app here are some of things to keep in mind:

- **Incorporate your business**
If you are looking to market your app under a business entity, then you will need to formally organize your company with your state's Secretary of State. The easiest incorporation type to form is the Limited Liability Company, which can often be done completely online. Depending on your funding model and your taxation preferences you may want to choose other incorporation types like an S-Corp. Nevertheless, you should spend the money and talk to a lawyer to see how you should legally organize your company.

- **Sign up for a developer account**
If you are building an iPhone app, you will need to create an Apple Developer account prior to being able to submit your app. Apple charges $99 per year for a developer account. Depending on the type of company you incorporate, signing up for an Apple Developer account can be done instantaneously or require you to fax in legal documents to Apple before it is approved. To release an app on Android, you will need a Google Play for Developers account. Google charges $25 per year for the developer account and requires you to provide the same type of legal documentation as Apple. Likewise, to release an app for the Windows Phone, you will need an active Windows Phone Developer account, which costs $99 a year.

- **Prepare appropriately sized App Icons and Screenshots**
When you submit to an app store, you will also need to provide at least one App Icon (usually in a couple of different sizes), which will graphically represent your app on a user's phone and in the app store. Additionally, you will usually need to provide at least 3 high-resolution screenshots of your app in action that will be visible in your app's listing on the marketplace. Instead of randomly snapping screenshots of your app, you should attempt to use the screenshots to demonstrate a coherent message about your app.

- **Finalize your App name, Tag line, Description and other marketing texts**

The listing you create for your app on a marketplace will be the public face of your app. You need to treat this listing as a giant billboard, as random people might stumble upon it and it's your app listing which will convince them whether to download your app or not. Thus, you need to think carefully about how to describe your app in its listing and the audience it's targeted towards. Generally, shorter is better, and you should keep your app listing as text light as possible. Coming up with a catchy tag line and equally effective app description is very hard and often takes weeks of revision until you land on something you might like. Thus, you should start preparing these texts long before you finish your development cycle.

- **Create marketing and support web site for your app**

While you can certainly create an app that doesn't have a web component, you will still need a very small web presence to release your app. When you submit an app to the Apple App Store Marketplace, you will be prompted to provide a URL users of your app can visit to get support for your app. There are no requirements for what must be on the web site beyond that the URL is valid and that your app is clearly the topic of the web site. Even a simple page with your app logo, and a brief description of what your app does should suffice.

We'll go into more detail into these areas along with other marketing tips later on in the book.

Getting through the Apple App Store Review Process

If you are building an iPhone app, then only one barrier stands between your app and the world: the Apple App Store Review. As we mentioned earlier in the book, one does not simply post their app on Apple's App Store Marketplace for the world to consume. To play in Apple's App Store Marketplace, your app needs to be approved by Apple.

Will the Gods of Cupertino give your app their blessing? Or will the Jobs-ian hammer fall and crush your dreams of Instagramsuccess? Nothing will put the kibosh on your app dreams quicker than a rejection by Apple. Luckily, getting passed the Apple App Store Review is actually fairly simple and is quite honestly something you shouldn't worry about as along you remember these three things:

1. Your app needs to pass the Uptight Citizen sniff test.

The Apple playground is a lot like Pleasantville. Those who control it don't take too well to sex, drugs, violence and copyrighted material anywhere inside of it, including inside of your app. (Hey, if you want to get all First Amendment about it, the Android room is just down the hall...) Before submitting your app, ask yourself this question: Would an Uptight Citizen be offended by anything in my app?

If your app allows users to submit and share photos, videos or other content with other users of the app, then you will need to show Apple that there is a mechanism in the app for removing objectionable and offensive material. Factor the design of such functionality into the plans for your first release.

2. Your app can't be crap.

Open your app and click a button. Does it crash? If so, then you have a crappy app.

Does your app UI consist largely of a white background with the odd UI control thrown down? You have a crappy app.

Does your app's layout look as if it were hand drawn by a 4-year old child? You have a crappy app.

The Crappy App bar is subjective at best, but you can look at Apple's recommended UI guidelines[21] to give you a better idea of what Apple might think one looks like. There is an entire industry of professional app developers releasing apps on the Apple App Store, so your app needs to stand side-by-side with the pros and not look like it was written by a Code Academy drop out.

3. Your app can't be hacked together.

Make sure whoever is writing the code for your app isn't using any private libraries or subverting the Apple operating system in anyway. Good engineers already know not to do it. Bad ones will look at you and go, "huh?" when you ask them if they are using any private libraries.

If your app uses any type of encryption (SSL, etc.), you will need to file an Encryption Registration Document with the U.S. Bureau of Industry and Security[22] before submitting to Apple. We're not joking., You can thank the US government for needing to jump through this Orwellian hoop. Going through the red tape can take up to a month, so plan ahead!

Don't try to get cute with Apple and subvert either the platform or try to go around the Export Control Rules; Apple will be able to tell immediately if you've done either.

The Apple App Store Review is a fairly straightforward process if you keep those three principles in mind. Of all the things to worry about in developing an app, the Apple App Store Review shouldn't be one of them. Do note that it does take Apple some time to review your app after you submit it. Typically, you should expect to wait 1 week after submitting your app before it will be reviewed and (hopefully) appear on the App Store.

Getting through the Google Play App Review Process

Unlike Apple, Google welcomes apps into its Google Play marketplace with widely stretched arms. Google does not enforce the strict content guidelines that Apple mandates and largely welcomes any type of app onto its marketplace. Google does perform some automated review of app code when it's submitted, however the Google review process is focused on ensuring apps aren't submitted which might steal sensitive data or install malware. As long you are building an app that isn't a virus or malware, you should expect the process of listing your app onto Google Play to be relatively quick and pain free.

Step 3: Release

Release Checklist: *If you are launching your first app here are some of things to keep in mind.*

1. Incorporate your business ☐

2. Sign up for a developer account ☐

3. Prepare appropriately sized App Icons, and Screenshots ☐

4. Finalize your App name, Tag line, Description and other marketing texts ☐

5. Reserve a domain name for your App web site ☐

6. Create a marketing and support web site for your App ☐

7. Familiarize yourself with analytics dashboards for tracking downloads, usage and reviews ☐

8. Submit your App ☐

Figure 51: While your app is in development, work through this checklist to ensure you are ready to submit when the app is finished

Step 4: Gather Feedback

Once you've released your app to the wild, your next step is to watch and learn how users react to your app and gain insight into what works and what doesn't work in your current version of the app. The commandment 'release early and often' is critically important, because you will only know how well your app is once it is in the hands of your customer. By drawing out your development milestones to include every feature you think is important and polish up every minor detail, you are leaving yourself open to the risk that all that effort would have been wasted if your customer doesn't like it. The truth of being a creator is that your opinion of what you build will certainly not be the same as the opinions of those who will use it. Thus, you need to get your app into the hands of your customer and then you need to watch, analyze, and draw conclusions to drive the direction of your app in the next release.

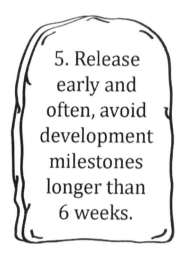

5. Release early and often, avoid development milestones longer than 6 weeks.

Figure 52: Use feedback from a release to guide development of the next release

There are a number of ways you can gather stats and other feedback from your users as they use your app. Here are a few metrics and tools you can use to track your app's growth and obtain user feedback:

App Store Reviews

Every major app marketplace provides a feedback mechanism where users can post comments and give a star rating to the apps they download. These comments are the clearest and most direct feedback you will get on your app from your user base. The rating your app gets from your users can have a dramatic effect on your download numbers, as users are likely to pass up an app with a marginal rating (e.g, 3 out of 5 stars) for a competitor with a much higher customer rating (e.g.,4.5 our of 5 stars). The app rating system serves as a very effective way to separate the bad apps from the good ones, and should be a strong incentive for you to not release a buggy app. Look at what people mention in your reviews: Do people complain that they are confused? Do they mention the app crashing or freezing? Generally, if more than one person mentions the same thing in any of your reviews, it is a sign of a problem you should address.

Download metrics

All of the major app marketplaces provide dashboards that show the number of downloads of your app over time. The number of downloads is the most basic metric you can use to gauge customer adoption of your app, although it does not provide much visibility beyond telling you the number of people that installed your app on a given day.

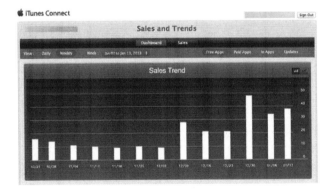

Figure 53: The iTunes Connect dashboard provides daily and weekly reports on download metrics

One interesting way you can use the download statistics is to measure the effectiveness of your marketing campaigns. Many app creators use social media to spread word about their apps. Using the number of downloads metric, you can track the 'bump' in

169

downloads you receive because of marketing activities. Depending on the type of marketing you are doing, you should be able to use this metric to measure and compare different channels for effectiveness. We'll discuss more about specific marketing tactics you can use for promoting your app later in the book.

Mobile Analytics

The most powerful way to track how users are using your app is to integrate your app with a mobile analytics package. *Mobile analytics* is a fancy term for instrumenting the code of your app to track and record the actions of users on it. This data is collected locally on users' phones and then transmitted to a central server where you can then perform analysis on the data.

The most popular analytics package is built by Flurry, which provides both the toolkit your developers will use to instrument the app and a very powerful analytics dashboard you can use to dissect and view the data. With Flurry, you can track metrics such as 'length of time in the app', 'the number of returning users vs. new users', 'average session length', etc. Additionally, you can define your own metrics to track the number of people using a certain function or the length of time users spend in each of your screens. This type of data is invaluable when planning further releases because it gives you much more granular visibility into people's behavior with your app.

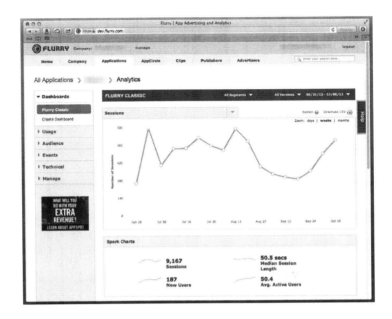

Figure 54: Flurry's analytics suite provides excellent insight into how users are using your app

Flurry provides client libraries that can be used by your developers to integrate Flurry instrumentation into iPhone, Android and Windows Phone apps. However, before your developer can integrate such metrics, you need to define the measurements you want to gauge in your app.

Step 4: Gather Feedback

Feedback Checklist: *Once you've released your app to the wild, your next step is to watch and learn how users react to your app and gain insight into what works and what doesn't work in your current version of the app. Here are a few metrics and tools you can use to track your app's growth and user feedback.*

1. App Store reviews, ratings and comments ☐

2. Download metrics, units and revenue ☐

3. Ad impressions, clicks and revenue *if applicable* ☐

4. Mobile analytics (ex. Flurry) for tracking usage metrics such as 'average session length' ☐

5. Web analytics (ex. Google Analytics) for tracking metrics and activity on your app's website ☐

6. Emails from your app's support contact ☐

Figure 55: Once released, ensure you keep track of these items to help understand how people are using your app

8

Concerning Engineers

Some people call them 'coders', while others like to use 'programmers' to describe them. The media likes to call them 'hackers', while some ultra-left wing environmentalists even use 'techno-fascists' to describe them. Companies like Google and Microsoft call them 'Software Development Engineers', while girls in high school probably called them something like 'spaz' or 'dweeb'. In the end, they are many names for those who write the mysterious 'code' which powers everything from the apps on your iPhone to the flight control systems on a Boeing 787. They are the craftsmen who will build your app.

In this chapter, let's take a step back from the world of apps and examine the world of software engineers. If you aren't planning on writing the code for your app yourself, then you need to be prepared to enter the domain of software engineers. Not only do you need to find and hire them for your project, but you also need to be able to understand and communicate with them. To hire the right engineer, you need to both understand a bit of their DNA and know what to look for in choosing the best one for your project. Over the course of the next few pages we will break through the technical divide and open up the world of the software engineer while giving you the tips and insight you need to be able to recruit and work alongside the best ones.

8.1

Finding the Right Kind For Your App

Building an app for a smartphone is a different beast than building a PC/Mac application. Like we have already explored, the great apps transition smoothly, always give the user visual cues when it's busy, and provide responsive user interface that never lags or is affected by what else the app might be doing. To build a great app, you need someone who will obsess about making sure all the tiny things that separate a great app from a good app get done. Finding someone who knows how to code isn't that hard; heck, investment bankers write thousands of lines of Visual Basic macro code, but that doesn't make them engineers. Ideally, you want to find a mobile engineer to build your app, someone who not only knows how to write code, but also understands how best to create an app for a 'post-PC' device.

For you, the most important job as it relates to programming your app is finding the right engineer to join your quest. The right engineer is not necessarily the grizzled veteran with 20 years of C++ experience. Neither is it the kid that's been hacking away at Ruby-on-Rails for a few months. The engineer you need isn't the brilliant savant who ruthlessly dissects and criticizes others' ideas because his are just that much better. The right engineer for your team is someone who is not only technically competent, but is also a person you can openly interchange ideas with, who shares your passion for the problem space, and has the curiosity to want to build your app.

What differentiates an engineer from a programmer is the thought they put into design of the app and the completeness of their work. A programmer can cobble code together to solve the immediate problem, but what about when your app has 1,000 users? An engineer approaches the problem from a long-term perspective and builds code from day one to achieve long-term goals. Good engineers won't write a line of code until they've understood all aspects of the problem and have sketched out a technical design for your app. You absolutely don't want someone to jump in and start hacking away code. Things like performance, scalability, localization and manageability are foundational to a good app and aren't usually something you can just worry about at a later time. If your engineer doesn't make the right design decisions at the very early stages of development, then you might have to start all over again when issues start to rise.

When recruiting engineers, you should focus less on the hard skills they have on their resume and more on the inter-personal dynamic you are able to establish with them. Think about it, you are going to be entering a very real relationship with them as your app moves from concept to production. You need to be able to communicate with your engineers such that they are able to understand your vision for the app and you are able to understand the technical issues that they might bring to your attention. This dynamic is critical. As our commandments state, your project will change as new things come up. You need to be able to work alongside your engineer to adapt.

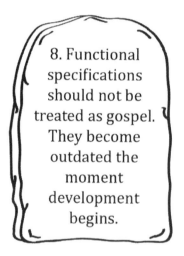

8. Functional specifications should not be treated as gospel. They become outdated the moment development begins.

Figure 56: Your app will change during development, you need an engineer who you can communicate with

Ideally, you want to work with a software engineer that has not only built mobile apps before, but has done so on the mobile platform you want your app to be built on. That is, if you are building an iOS app, then you want to find an engineer who has at least built one iOS app. While an Android developer will probably be able to pick up iOS with little difficulty, it's likely that your project will take much longer to complete as the engineer comes up to speed on the iOS platform. Generally, you can expect it to take 1 month for an experienced mobile engineer to come up to speed with a new mobile platform. While they are doing so, you can expect progress on your app to be slow. It is entirely possible you won't be able to find an engineer that has the experience with the platform you want to build on. If this happens to you, then your next best bet is to find a mobile engineer who has built apps on any other major platform.

If you are unable to find a mobile engineer at all, only then you should look to hiring a non-mobile software engineer to work on your app. The downside to hiring a software engineer that doesn't have experience building mobile apps is that they will not be aware of the idiosyncrasies involved in building for mobile. However, the advantage they have is that many of the same languages and frameworks that are used to build desktop applications are also used to build mobile apps. For instance, the same language (C#) and framework (.NET) used to build apps for Windows Phone is used to build many Windows applications and websites, especially in large corporations. Thus, a software engineer who has built desktop applications using .NET & C# already knows much of what they'd need to know to build an app on the Windows Phone platform. Likewise, an engineer who can build applications for the Mac operating system already knows the language (Objective-C) and framework (Cocoa) that is at the heart of building an iOS app. Instead of spending the first few weeks of development learning the language and platform, these engineers will need to ramp on mobile application design and how they differ from desktop applications.

In any case, experience is the mother of all differentiators for software engineers. If you meet a software engineer who has been in the business for 15 years, but doesn't know how to build a mobile app, that's still worlds better than someone who has only been coding for 1 year but entirely on mobile apps. The funny thing about software engineering is that there is a lot of repetition in its design. After a while, most design problems or bugs that come up will be something an experienced engineer will have already encountered. An experienced engineer who might not know the language of mobile apps or have never even used a smartphone will still be able to leverage much of their knowledge and experience if they were to embark on building a mobile app.

8.2

Identifying the Good Ones

While the constitution provides that all men are created equal, the same is not true for software developers. How do you identify a quality software engineer versus a lazy programmer? Even if you don't know a lick of code, there are some straightforward things you can look for to evaluate an engineer and their ability:

- **Ask to see a portfolio of previous work**

If you are talking to an independent engineer then they should be able to provide references to apps they have built either for themselves or for other clients. These references should be links to published apps on any of the major app marketplaces. Try a few of them out and try to assess how well the apps look and feel. Does the app crash? Is the app slow? Are the graphics properly sized? The quality of an engineer's past work is indicative to the quality they'd bring to your app.

- **Have a conversation with them about something non-technical**

As we mentioned earlier in the chapter, you want an engineer who can communicate well and who you feel comfortable interacting with. You'll find engineers who run the entire gamut of social awareness: from the introverted recluse, to the gregarious and personable. Pick a non-technical topic and ask for their opinion on it. Are they articulate? Can they think through a topic that isn't tech related and still form an intelligent viewpoint? Are they open to feedback?

- **Google them!**

This is the most basic due diligence you should do for any engineering prospect. If an engineer has listed in their experience a software engineer role at another company, verify that! Less important is the company they worked for and more important is the position they were in. Note, unless their title included 'developer,' 'engineer,' or 'programmer,' it is unlikely that their role was a software engineering position.

- **Look at what projects they do on their own time**
A mark of a good engineer is a desire to build, even if it's only for personal use or as part of an open source initiative. Today, many developers use GitHub (http://www.github.com) to manage the source code for projects they are working on. GitHub is an online source code repository that has social networking functionality that allows you to look at the projects a developer is currently working on and their own contributions to them. Ask engineers for their GitHub usernames and browse through their profiles. See how many projects they are a part of, and use the 'Public Activity' section to see how frequently they contribute source code changes. A busy GitHub account indicates that an engineer is involved writing code for projects outside of work.

- **See how involved they are in developer forums**
When someone is writing code and runs into an issue they are unable to solve, they usually turn to developer forums on the Internet to help find a solution. The most popular of such forums is Stack Overflow (http://www.stackoverflow.com). Stack Overflow is a website where people ask and answer on a wide range of programming related questions. Users of the site earn reputation points and status for each 'up-vote' an answer they provide gets from other users. Stack Overflow has become the go-to site for getting programming help because there are so many engineers willing to help answer other people's questions. Ask a potential hire if they have a Stack Overflow account, and then look at their user profile online. Are they an active participant? How well-written are their answers? If they answer a lot of questions within a single topic and those answers receive a lot of up-votes, then they probably know what they are talking about. Generally, its good sign to see an engineer actively participate in online forums, as it is indicative of both a helping manner and deep technical knowledge.

8.3

Herding Cats: Tips on Managing Them

We've both lived with and breathed alongside programmers of all ages, skill levels and degrees of social ability. From the countless hours spent at computer labs in school to massive development projects at Microsoft, we've learned that managing software engineers is like herding cats - really intelligent and often highly opinionated cats. While in social circles a programmer might seem insecure and unsure of himself, put them in front of a keyboard and they will not hesitate to call you and your ideas 'stupid'. For a myriad of reasons, from some having sand kicked in their face as a kid to others' desires to be the smartest person in the room, software engineers can be notoriously difficult to manage. Combine this with the overwhelming advantage in technical knowledge that they have and you have the recipe for a project management disaster if you aren't prepared to handle it.

Let's explore some tips and lessons to help you manage a development team:

Embrace being the dumbest person in the room

If you are to manage a team of engineers, then accept that you are the dumbest person in the room. For MBAs, this could be a tough pill to swallow, but swallow it you must. You need to lead the engineers building your app, but you need to do it from a business perspective and what is best for the growth of your enterprise. Your role in leading the development of your app is much like that of a Program Manager (PM) at a software company like Microsoft. A PM's job is to manage small teams of engineers to build features as part of a larger software release. PMs are usually not technical and generally focus on ensuring their project is finished on-time and is aligned with the business goals of the company. Good PMs had developers that would walk through fire for them even when they knew next to nothing technically. The bad PMs had developers who would ignore them at best and be openly hostile towards them at worst. Bad PMs became nothing more than glorified assistants, spending their time writing redundant status mails and scheduling meetings that nobody attended. Meanwhile, the developers were off in their corner building whatever they wanted to, which is a very bad place for your project to be in.

What makes a good PM has little to do with their technical depth and more to do with their ability to guide their team to the right answers by asking the right questions. The good PMs never asserted their authority and instead played the role of student to the engineers when it came to technical issues. The good PMs rarely made bold pronouncements and instead acted like a debate moderator, with the engineers playing the role of the candidates. A good PM knew that their engineers were smart enough to get to the right answer to solve technical issues, and that they just needed to pave the road by asking the right questions.

Embrace the role of being the dumbest person in the room: ask questions, listen to the answers, and keep probing. Engineers are quick to dismiss those who they perceive to be batting out of their league, so play little league, accept you know nothing, and go from there.

You Own the Vision of Your App, You Need to Direct the Ship

Computer programming by its very nature requires a programmer to apply cold logic to solve each problem presented to them. In programming, everything is rational and every command issued to the computer is the result of some series of logical operations that preceded it. Knowing this, it's not hard to see how after a few years of programming 16 hours a day that a developer might begin to approach every situation with the same cold logical precision. This is great if you are a prosecutor in a criminal trial, but few problems in life can and should be objectively solved. When it comes to shipping software, you will have to make decisions that are subjective and not completely logical. Your app will have holes, it will have bugs and it might not always work. You have to be pragmatic in what you build and fix. Programmers are not always pragmatic, and many would gladly delay shipping a piece of software to fix or redesign internal components all for the sake of appeasing their own desire for everything to make sense.

You have to be the voice of reality on your team; your job is to be the keeper of the vision of the app. Your engineers are little machines of productivity looking to solve every problem they can find. You have to make sure that they are always solving the right problems. You are like the guy at the front of the boat in Ben Hur, beating the drum as programmers row the oars (minus the master-slave relationship of course!) Nobody expects you to be able to row; you just need to make sure that everyone is rowing in the same direction.

A great way to find yourself with a failed app is to sit idly by while letting engineers dictate what needs to be built. When an engineer tells you, "Our performance sucks! We must redesign the database!" you should take pause. You might not know what a database is, and that's ok. What you need to know is what constitutes acceptable performance? When an engineer says, "performance sucks," you should ask, "How slow is it?" and "How that will affect the user experience?" Many times the engineers are right and performance is too slow to release, but don't accept redesigning the database to be the only way to fix it. Remember that programmers rarely advocate the 'quick and dirty' solution and would instead rather do the 'right' thing according to them. Ask the engineer the right questions, such as:

- Is 'redesigning the database' the only way to speed it up?
- How long will it take to 'redesign the database'?
- Is there functionality we can change to help speed it up?
- Can we adjust our assumptions to enable a cheaper fix?

Note that none of these questions have anything to do with the technical specificities of a database. Instead, you are asking the questions that will most likely fire up the engineer's brain. When an engineer sees a problem, they might only see a technical solution. However, changing your assumptions or adjusting functionality can solve many technical challenges. It's up to you to find those answers.

Buffer, Buffer, Buffer

Software engineers are confident. You'll rarely meet a software engineer who hems and haws at their ability to complete a task, even if they have never solved that problem before. That confidence isn't misplaced; given enough time a good software developer will surmount whatever new problem they put their mind to. While programmers are great problem solvers, they are terrible estimators of time. When a programmer gives you a time estimate they do so based on what they see as being the problem, not the iceberg that lies underneath the surface. Take our word for it; every piece of software is a giant under-the-surface iceberg lying in wait for a programmer to run right on top of. It's not the programmer's fault bugs and slowdowns happen. It's the nature of the beast. Most of the time there is no avoiding the issues once you hit them and you have to wait for the engineer to get through them.

Instead of pulling your hair out when delays push back your ship date, you ought to prepare your schedules to take these things happening into account. The process of taking an estimate and adding in additional to time to handle unknowns is called *buffering*. When you buffer your schedule, you are building in extra time that is to be used as a cushion to handle unexpected delays that come up during development.

When you ask for an estimate from your developer to complete a task, you'll usually receive an estimate measured in 'days'. A good rule of thumb for buffering is to take these estimates and multiply it by a buffer-factor (>1). The buffer factor you pick should represent the technical risk of what is being estimated. If the developer is confident in their ability to deliver a component on-schedule, then you should pick a lower number like 1.20. The more technical risk or uncertainty in an estimate, the greater the buffer factor you should use. If you find yourself using a factor greater than 2, then you should really ask your developer to give you a better estimate.

Don't Tell Your Engineers about Your Buffers

Buffering is key to making your development schedule stick. But buffering should not be taken by engineers to be time available for them to use, because then you will just need to buffer again! Buffer is an emergency reserve that is meant to bail out the engineers when they think they have run out of time. You ever notice when your car's fuel tank hits 'E', your car doesn't run out of gas? The car manufacturers have built in reserves into the fuel tank, and they purposely don't tell you it's there. If you knew there were two notches worth of fuel available below the 'E' line, then you would continue driving and ultimately end up running out of gas. In the same vein, engineers will take all the time you give them. You need to place hard deadlines that engineers believe to be unshakeable and must be met. Having a hard, fixed deadline motivates engineers to work when they could instead be reading Reddit or playing Foosball. If you tell them you have buffered three weeks into the schedule, we guarantee you that they will operate already assuming that the deadline has been extended to include those three weeks.

Hold your schedule close to your chest and maintain an internal buffer that you temper all deadline estimates with. For everyone else there is only one deadline, and that deadline is the deadline until the last possible minute. When you need to use your buffer, do not use it all at once. Instead, use only a few days of it at a time and leave some of it in the cupboard. Extending your deadline by 5 days is much better than extending it 21 days, as it keeps the intensity up and keeps everybody in a shipping mode.

Let Them Work!

At Microsoft, it was difficult for engineers to get stuff done on time because of an endless parade of meetings and other distractions that took them away from programming. Studies have shown that, on average, it takes a programmer 20-30 minutes to fully engage a difficult programming problem after starting it. Only after this time is an engineer truly productive and able to make good progress. The minute they are distracted by some outside interference, they are reset and have that same 20-30 minute uphill climb before they regain their productivity. If you have something to ask your engineers, email them. Don't just disturb them to ask the question. In fact, unless your building is on fire, or Cloverfield is running loose outside, never disrupt your programmers while they work.

When it comes to meetings, avoid them if you can. If you must schedule them, make sure they are early in the day and done prior to the engineers engaging in their activities. Your job is to be the guardian of your engineers; you need to shield them from the world and the distractions that come with it. If you don't know the answer to a question, instead of asking the engineer for the answer you should tell the person asking that you'll get back to them. If your engineers are hungry and need food, then you should go get it for them. Much of your job day-in and day-out will be to create an environment where your engineers can work and remain productive.

Don't Accumulate Too Much Technical Debt

Software is time consuming to build right. An app can easily take six months of work to be finished. While you might have a fire underneath you to get it to the market, you have to balance delivering it on time and building a product that works. Early on in the development process it's easy to say, "Take the shortcut, we'll come back and fix it." Be very wary of this thought process, as software is not something that you can easily go back and fix. Every time you cut a corner by hardcoding a behavior, or taking a simpler yet more inefficient solution, you accumulate *technical debt*.

Technical debt is the future effort you are signing up for when you cut a corner in the short-term. Be very cognizant of what it means to fix something in the future and how much effort that will take. Like residential mortgages, not all-technical debt is created the same and some types are especially toxic. When it comes to issues that will impact your ability to scale your app to thousands of users, be extremely wary. If you expect your app to be the next DrawSomething or Angry Birds, understand that means you will need to support tens of thousands of people using your app, potentially at the same time. When you cut corners on the scalability of your app, you are setting yourself up for failure. Most startups fail not because their product wasn't liked, but rather they attempted to scale up too quickly and their processes and technology couldn't keep up. Don't let this be you.

9

Marketing Your App

Your journey through the Appverse doesn't end when your app is released. In reality, your journey has just begun. Many people enter the app process with a 'Field of Dreams' mentality of *if you build it, they will come*. That is, as long as you build a great app, people will find it. As two people who used to believe this, we attest that it is far from the truth. The reality many Appsters face after spending months and thousands of dollars to release an app is having very few people download it upon release. Apps don't discover themselves. Just because you've created an amazing app doesn't mean anyone will use it. Building a great app is only part of your journey; you then need to market it! There are over 800,000 apps on the Apple App Store. Just because you've built an amazingly useful app doesn't mean anyone will ever try it unless you find a way to market it to them.

At this point of the book we have already covered much of what it takes to design and build a great app. In this chapter, we are going to delve into the little known yet hugely important area of app marketing. If you are building a free app, you need to know how to scale it up with lots of users, while at the same time not over extending the technical limit of your app. If you are building a revenue-generating product, then you need to know which marketing channels to use to get people to download and buy your product. In this chapter, we will outline the basics of app marketing and equip you with the knowledge you need to ensure that when your app is released there is a ready and waiting audience to download it.

9.1

Setting User Acquisition Goals

The scope of whom you market your app to needs to evolve along with the app itself. In your first few beta releases, marketing means finding test users who are willing to suffer through the bugs and incompleteness of the app and can give you constructive feedback on what works and what doesn't. Usually, this means friends and family. However, you can create a limited outreach campaign where you seek out early adopters who might not know you, but are willing to take a chance and try out something new.

A good place to market your app while it's in beta is through BetaLi.st (http://www.betali.st), an online community that showcases products that are in the beta phases and not yet ready for general use. If you can get your app featured on a site like BetaLi.st, you will be attracting a targeted group of customers who are seeking out beta products to use.

While your app is still in its beta releases, you shouldn't make a big marketing splash to try and get the general public to download your app. Far from helping your app, this could actually hurt you in the long term. If you invite people to use your app before its ready, you risk delivering a bad experience to the users and pushing them away forever. Mobile app users are a very fickle bunch. If your app opens up and crashes or has a lot of bugs, chances are users won't open it again. You might find that by creating a huge push for downloads of your apps in the beta phases will ultimately end up alienating your user base.

Once your app has moved out of beta and is publically available, you want to gradually increase the number of people you are reaching with your marketing efforts. Unless you've been able to test your app's technical infrastructure with thousands of users during your beta releases, a huge increase in the number of users of your app in a very short time can be very dangerous. You may end up getting thousands of downloads, but if your app's backbone can't handle the strain of all the additional users, you again risk alienating your customers and never being able to recover.

Instead of blindly attempting to gain additional downloads of your app, a better approach to growing your app is working with your engineers and setting user acquisition goals at a per month or quarterly basis. This conversation needs to happen with your engineers because given a desired number of users, they should be able to gauge how well the technical infrastructure would be able to handle the increased load. Further, by setting user acquisition goals through a 12-18 month period, you will give your engineers the time needed to prepare and test the app to handle future load. So while your app might not be able to handle 10,000 users on the day of its first release, given six months of lead-time, your engineers should be able to verify and prepare for it.

Once you've set goals for the growth of your app over the short to medium term, you can then devise your strategy for promoting your app and acquiring users on it.

9.2

The Basics

When you list your app on a marketplace like the Apple App Store or Google Play, your main interaction point with potential customers will be the listing page created for your app on the marketplace. When people want to download your app, they will go to your app's marketplace page that contains the following information:

1. App name
2. App icon
3. Description of your app
4. Screenshots of your app
5. Publisher information (links to your web site, along with a link to a support URL for the app)
6. Content ratings (is your app R-rated or just PG-13?)
7. Customer reviews

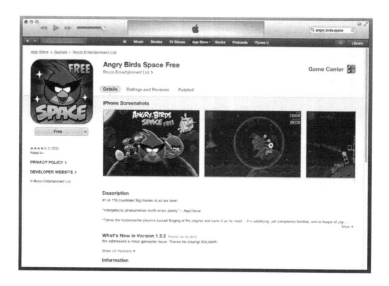

Figure 57: Apple App Store listing for Angry Birds

Figure 58: Google Play listing for Angry Birds

Figure 59: Windows Phone Store listing for Angry Birds

When someone uses the marketplace's search functionality to look for apps, they are displayed a list of search results for apps that match what they were searching for. In this search result list, they will see three pieces of information for each app: the name, the app icon, and a customer review rating. The combination of these three pieces of information will either cause the user to click and visit your app listing page or ignore it entirely. Every person who will download your app will eventually arrive at your app's page on the marketplace, thus making it the most important marketing asset you have. Your goal for deciding what you put on your listing page is to create enough of a hook to compel the user looking at the page to download and try your app. Let's explore some of what goes into your app listing and how you can optimize it to gain more users:

Naming Your App

Picking a name for your app will be one of the toughest decisions you will make; one you should not leave till the last minute. Beyond being used to identify your app, the name of your app is also an opportunity to convey what the app does to a potential customer.

If you are building a utility app, a good strategy is to choose a name that in some way includes the problem you are trying to solve, along with an app icon that presents an equally obvious picture. When people are looking to download an app to solve a particular problem, they will typically search for that problem through the marketplace search function (e.g., 'to do list apps', or 'cookbooks'). Ask yourself what people might type to search for your app and try to incorporate those keywords into the name of your app. Then, create an app icon, which, combined with your app, name makes it very clear to anyone browsing through a list of apps what your app does. A good example of this type of naming is the Flashlight app. As the name implies, this is an app that turns your phone into a flashlight by turning on the camera flash. When you search for 'Flashlight' on the Apple App Store, you see the following listing:

Figure 60: Marketplace listing page for the Flashlight app

194

It's pretty obvious from the combination of the app name, the app icon and the screenshot what this app does. For utility apps, try to avoid esoteric or abstract names and focus on keeping it simple and obvious because people will generally be looking for them by describing the problem they want to solve.

However, once you move outside of utility apps, the naming conventions for apps is much less obvious. In general, the less your app has to do with solving a real problem, the greater the freedom you have to choose whatever name you'd like for the app. We don't prescribe to any belief that there are rules to what makes a good app name, so let your creativity run wild and call your app whatever name you think fits. But before you decide on a name, search for it on Google and see what comes up. If the name you picked already has numerous results for other sites and services, it's probably not a good choice. Beyond potential trademark issues, you will fight an uphill battle to get your app to be the first result returned by Google when people search for it. People need to be able to find your app on Google, something they won't be able to do if it's buried at the bottom of the search page.

Also, before picking a name, you need to check whether there is a domain name available. As we mentioned earlier in the book, there are a number of clever ways to modify the name of your app in order to find an available domain. Try seeing if you can morph the name of your app to take advantage of new and popular domain suffixes like *.ly* or *.me*. No matter what name you pick for your app, make sure you can reserve a domain to exactly match the app name.

Creating Engaging App Descriptions

Once someone clicks on your app in the marketplace and lands upon your app listing, the next piece of information they will see is the app description. As you might surmise, the app description is prose you write when submitting your app that serves to explain your app to anybody viewing your listing. Writing an engaging app description is crucial to getting someone to pull the trigger to download your app.

Your app description can be as long as you'd like, but note that most people won't read more than a few sentences before they either download it or leave your app page. Also note that in the Apple App Store, the first five lines of your app description will be visible immediately when someone visits your app listing, but the rest of your prose will be hidden under a 'more' link that people will need to click on to expand. Therefore, it's critical that the first five lines of your app description convey a clear message to the user about what your app does and why they should download it.

Figure 61: Flashlight, notice the text above the 'more' button

A good app description reads more like an advertisement than a bulleted list of features. While it is tempting to enumerate everything your app can do in its description, it's far more effective to write a short description of your app that very succinctly pitches it to the customer. If you want to include a bullet list of features, put them near the end of your description so that they are below the fold and only seen when a user presses the 'more' button on your listing.

Marketplace Customer Reviews

All major mobile app marketplaces contain some notion of customer reviews, usually measured on a scale of 1 to 5 stars. Outside of any marketing buzz you are able to create yourself, the reviews your app receives on the marketplace will be the primary way potential customers will choose between it and competing apps. It is critical to the success of your app that it receives a high review rating; otherwise it is a very clear sign to customers that the app is either buggy or not very good. Once a negative review appears on your app page, there is very little you can do to remove it beyond hoping to bury it with newer reviews. Thus, you need to protect your app's review score and actively recruit friends, families and users of your app to come back to the marketplace and submit positive reviews.

Furthermore, your app's visibility within the marketplace is dictated by the reviews it receives. Both the Apple App Store and Google Play feature select apps on their front pages that dramatically increase the exposure the selected apps receive. In order to be featured, your app needs to have not just a very high average review score, but also an equally high number of reviews submitted. Also, if you can get a large number of positive reviews to be submitted for your app in a short period of time, it increases the chances of your app being featured as it conveys rapidly increasing popularity to the marketplace organizers.

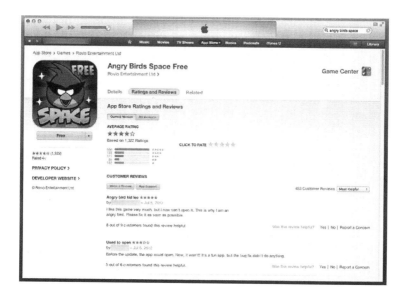

Figure 62: Marketplace reviews are critically important to your app's success

People are lazy, and unless you ask them to review your app, or if your app really angers them, they won't write reviews. You could create a great app that most people love, but the only review you might receive would be from the one person that your app crashed on. An effective way to increase the number of reviews your app receives is to integrate prompts into the app itself that remind people after a certain number of days to submit a review. It's very easy to have this functionality included in your app, as numerous open-source libraries exist, such as Appirater (https://github.com/arashpayan/appirater), which prompts users to rate and review your app.

9.3

Leverage the Web to Promote Your App

Unless you are building a utility app, only a small number of people will find out about your app by perusing the app marketplace and stumbling upon it. Instead, you need to create buzz and drive people to the marketplace to download your app. No matter where it is in the development process, you can leverage the web and social media to build awareness of your app and cultivate demand. The easiest, most effective way to do this is by building a website to promote your app. In doing so, you'll create a central landing site that anyone can come to and which you own. While the listing page you create on the marketplace can serve this role, creating your own web site gives you complete control of its look and feel, in addition to being able to build demand for your app through traditional Internet marketing. Let's take a look at how you can put the web to use to promote your app.

Build an App Website

No matter what, your app marketing efforts should start with a dedicated web site to showcase and promote your app. By having a website, you will not only be able to drive traffic to your app's listing on the marketplace, but you will also be able to measure and analyze the effectiveness of your marketing efforts. A drawback to the marketplace listings it that they do not give you visibility into how many people visit the listing, where they come from and who they are. The only metric app marketplaces tend to provide is the number of people who end up downloading your app. This by itself is not enough information to measure the effectiveness of your marketing efforts. By having a website, and using a web analysis tool, like Google Analytics, to analyze its traffic, you will gain invaluable insight into the traffic patterns to and from your app.

Furthermore, with a website, you will be able to build brand power of your app by increasing the visibility of the app web site in search engines through the use of Search Engine Optimization (SEO) and Search Engine Marketing (SEM) techniques (We'll cover more on these two concepts later on in the chapter). The more relevant traffic you can drive to your marketing website, then presumably the greater number of downloads you will be able to generate.

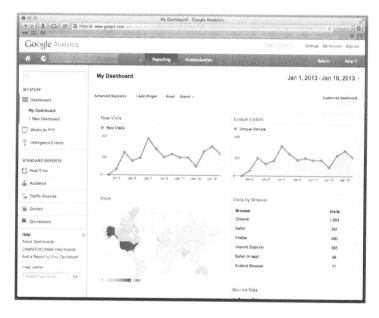

Figure 63: Google Analytics allows you to perform deep analysis on traffic arriving at your app's web site

Creating a website for your app is actually simple; you can probably do it yourself!

One of the easiest and most popular ways to setup a homepage is to use the popular blogging tool Wordpress. Wordpress is a free platform you can download that makes creating a web site very simple. The power of Wordpress is that it is an open source platform with a very healthy ecosystem of plugins and themes developed for it by people across the world. Themes are pre-packaged bits of Wordpress configuration that style your web site to look a certain way. Plugins are pieces of logic that plug in to

Wordpress that enable you to do things like track visitor statistics through Google and optimize search engine visibility for your site. If you are building a website for your app, you can purchase a pre-built theme designed specifically for marketing iPhone apps, such as Templatic's iPhone/Android App Wordpress Theme (http://templatic.com/members/go.php?r=41694&i=133). Once you install this on your website, it's a matter of filling in the various text boxes with your app descriptions and uploading a few screenshots and voila: instant app website! The beauty of Wordpress is that in most cases, you can make a beautiful marketing-optimized web site without knowing a lick of HTML code.

Once you've created a web site for your app, you then need to decide what content should be on it. Your app web site is a promotional tool for your app, so ideally it should be a single page web site that gives visitors and immediate sense of what your app is and why they should be interested in it. If your app is still in development or in a closed beta program, then use your web site as a promotional vehicle to build awareness of the upcoming release of your app. If your app has been released and is available on the app marketplace, your app web site can also be used to sign people up for your app and to then direct them to the app marketplace to downloadit. Additionally, you can use additional pages on your website to provide support, post public notices about bugs and any other news about your app.

Figure 64: The Templatic iPhone App Wordpress theme lets you easily create a web page to promote your app

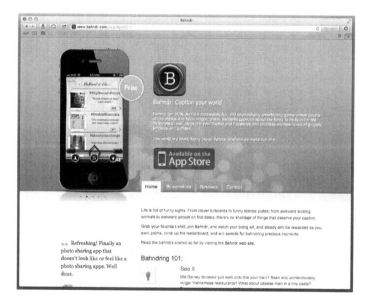

Figure 65: By changing the options on Templatic's iPhone App Theme you can create an app web page in very little time

Create a Promotional Video

If your app is still in beta, then the goal of your web site should be to stoke demand for your app. At the very least, you should have a simple text description of your app on your web site. However, a more effective promotional tool is to create a video for your app and host it on your web site, Facebook and YouTube for people to view. Don't look at the video as just a demo of your app, but use it as a way of promoting your app in an entertaining and engaging way.

The best promotional videos are those which are themselves entertaining. A great example of a promotional video is one released by the startup a Dollar Shave Club (http://www.youtube.com/watch?v=ZUG9qYTJMsI). This video was created as part of Dollar Shave Club's fundraising campaign on the social fundraising site Kickstarter. The video they created is both hilarious and informative, and ended up gaining huge amounts of press for the startup as the video quickly went viral. Anyone can create a video, and getting one professionally produced can be done for about $1,000. Videos as a medium are more accessible to people and are likely to provide much more information to the viewer than what you'd put in text. Furthermore, videos make for great social media content. Plus, there is always the chance your video will go viral! (More on viral marketing later on in the chapter)

Establish a Social Media Footprint

Social media is a great platform to build awareness of your app, whether it's in development or already released. The goal with your social media marketing efforts is to attract people to your app, and then build a relationship with them through a narrative based on the posts you make. Both Facebook and Google+ offer very easy ways for you to create a dedicated Page for your app. Through these pages, you can start building conversations around your app by simply posting status updates on your app's page informing people of your development schedule, upcoming releases or newsworthy events.

Your social media outreach is only as effective as the number of people you can get to 'Like' or 'Follow' your page. To get more people to 'Like' or 'Follow' your app on social media, you need to create entertaining, shareable content. Remember the promotional video we mentioned in the last paragraph? Well it turns out videos make for great sharable content, in addition to being ideally suited for distribution through a Facebook or Google+ page. Instead of creating a single promotional video for your app, you can make a series of shorter videos that document the progress of your app from design to release.

If videos aren't your thing, then use your app web site to host a blog. Every post you create for the blog makes for a unique piece of content you can share through Google, Facebook and Twitter. The more you share, the greater the awareness of your app will grow. You can measure the impact and effectiveness of your social media campaign by using Google Analytics to analyze how many visitors came to your site and became aware of your app because of these posts.

Use Email to Communicate With Your Customers

Irrespective if you use video or simply text to promote your app prior to release, your web site should be collecting email addresses of people who visit and are interested in your app. Ask any internet advertiser and they will tell you that the single most valuable piece of information you can collect from your web site's visitors is their email address. With an email, you can build a relationship with your prospective customers by keeping them up to date on your development status and instructing them to download the app once it comes out. To help you manage your email marketing campaigns, you can use a service like MailChimp.com that makes it easy to design email templates and manage their distribution to your audience. Furthermore, with MailChimp you can analyze the effectiveness of your emails and gain insight on how many people are opening them and clicking on links.

9.4

Building an Audience for Your App

Promotional vehicles serve little value if you are unable to get anybody to visit your website or to download your app. Once you've created a web site for your app, you then need to make sure people are able to find it through search engines like Google and Bing. On the Internet, search engine visibility is king when it comes to promoting a web site or product. Having your app listed near the top of the first page of search results can be the deciding factor between your app and a competitor.

Marketing through search comes in two varieties: Search Engine Optimization (SEO) and Search Engine Marketing (SEM). SEO is about improving your app's visibility in Google search results whenever someone searches for keywords that are relevant to your app. SEO deals exclusively with organic search result links, that is, non-sponsored links that you do not pay Google for. The other end of the coin is SEM, which is marketing your app through paid advertising displayed when people search for keywords on Google or when users visit Google-affiliated sites. Depending on the type of app you are building, you'll use one, or both, of these techniques to drive more traffic to your web site and app.

Figure 66: A Google search results page is made of a variety of paid (SEM) and organic (SEO) results

SEO: Building Organic Awareness for Your App

When you search for something on Google you are presented with a set of search results that include sponsored advertisements (usually placed along the top and sides of the search results page) and a list of regular links. The regular links are displayed in order of how relevant Google thinks they are based on what you typed into the search box. SEO is all about increasing Google's judgment of your app's relevance to a targeted set of search terms (keywords).

Google became the dominant search engine on the Internet because the algorithm it uses is able to judge how relevant a web site is to a particular search term by indexing the content of the site and by analyzing the links from other web sites that point to it. When analyzing inbound links to a site, Google looks at both the structure of the link text (what keywords are in the link?) and also the source of the link (how credible is the web site that is linking?) to determine how relevant a web site is to a particular set of search keywords. Improving your site's SEO rankings is a difficult, time-consuming task because the only way to do so is by increasing the number of credible websites that link to your site. Since you do not own these other sites, you will need to convince whoever does that your app is important and deserves to be listed on their site.

Imagine you are building a task management app. You will want your app and website to rank at or near the top of Google search queries that contain the keywords 'iPhone to-do list app'. The absolute first step to get your web site to be returned for that query is to ensure that your website has the right metadata attached to it that tells Google, "Hey, this is a site for an iPhone to-do list app."

Metadata is a fancy term for information embedded in your website that Google is able to read and from which it is able to understand what is on the site. The metadata in this case are HTML elements that embedded within the header section of a website (i.e. the section of HTML code that begins with <head>). For any web site you visit it's very easy to see what metadata they publishing. If you are using Chrome: right click on any web site, and click 'View Source'. This will bring up a screen filled with HTML code. Look for HTML tags that start with <meta> and that's the metadata we are talking about.

Having the right metadata attached to your site will only get you so far with Google. You also need to make sure the content of your site actually has something to do with 'iPhone to-do list app'. If you use your web site to host a blog about your app, where you write blog posts talking about the different features of your task management app, along with general conversation about task management apps for the iPhone, the Google algorithm will see this and then start to automatically return your web site in search results that contain 'iPhone to-do list app'. However, at the start, it's likely that your website will be so deeply buried in the returned search results that very few people will actually see it.

To improve the ranking of your web site in Google's search results, you need to embark on the second and much more difficult aspect of SEO: getting other web sites to link to your page. If your task management app has a link from a TechCrunch article with the words, "X is a great to-do list app for the iPhone" in it, then Google will likely judge your app to be highly relevant to people searching for 'to-do list iPhone app'. If your site has a link from a Tumblr site that your friend put up that contains the text "X is the best to-do list app on the iPhone," Google will score that much lower than the TechCrunch link because Google trusts the

207

TechCrunch website to be a much more trustworthy source than a random Tumblr site.

The crux of SEO is getting other established web sites to link to your site using keywords that are relevant to your app. The process of getting these links is called *link building*. There are many different strategies to link building and SEO in general. What we've presented thus far is a gross simplification of an entire industry that exists to help people rank their websites better. There are legions of independent SEO consultants and websites that provide knowledge and tools to help webmasters approach the problem of SEO. If you want to learn more about SEO techniques, a good place to start is by reading the SEO blog at SEOMoz.com.

In the meantime, let's take a closer look at link building and how you can use it to promote your app.

Strategies for Link Building

Link building refers to the process of reaching out to well established web sites and obtaining links from those sites to either your app's marketplace listing or dedicated website. The more of these links you can get to your website, the more traffic that will come to it as Google recognizes the increased popularity of your site. However, not all links are created equal and you want to ensure that you build the right type of links, as bad links (i.e. obviously fraudulent links on low-quality websites) will hurt your site's ranking. Here are some things you need to consider when building links to your web site:

The PageRank (PR) of the site giving the link. A website's PR is the score given to it by Google (between 0-10) that measures the its importance. A site that has many high-quality links pointing to it will have a higher PR than one without. The higher the PR of the site linking to your website, the greater PR impact it will have on your site.

You want to build 'follow' links. A hyperlink is represented in HTML by an anchor tag which looks something like this:

```
<a href="http://www.yoururl.com">text that describes the link</a>
```

This is a normal link that Google will count towards your site's

PR. However, some web sites do not want the links that appear on their sites to be evaluated by Google (to prevent spam linking), and they attach a 'no-follow' attribute to the anchor tag:

```
<a rel="nofollow" href="http://www.yoururl.com">text that describes
the link</a>
```

No-follow links provide zero SEO value to your site. Many web sites and forums only allow no-follow links, so you should not waste your time attempting to link-build with them, as they will not provide any SEO benefit to your site.

You want the text in the hyperlink to contain important keywords that describe your site. When Google comes across a hyperlink in a website, it uses the keywords that are contained within the link to categorize the site. If you were building a to-do list app, then you would want links that point to your site to contain words like 'to-do list app' or 'iPhone task management app,' etc.

Link building is tough. You need to get other web sites to post content that links to your site. However, with some elbow grease and persistence, you can steadily improve the SEO ranking of your web site by launching a sustained link-building campaign. Here are some popular ways to build links to your app's web site:

- **Guest blogging**

One of the tried and true ways of building links to your app and web site is by guest blogging. Guest blogging is just like what it sounds: you write articles on other people's blogs. In exchange for writing a blog post, you are generally able to include links back to your own site in the author byline or directly in the post. Guest blogging works because you are creating quality content for another site and quality content is always in demand. The relationships you build with other web masters are key to guest blogging, and you want to post on blogs that have high enough PageRanks that the links back to your site improve your rankings. As an Appster, you might want to find other app news and review sites where you could contribute a guest blog post. A popular web site to find other bloggers looking for people to write guest blogs is MyBlogGuest.com (http://www.myblogguest.com). This is a free community where bloggers exchange articles and find people looking for guest bloggers.

209

- **Forum posts**

Forums are online communities where discuss topics and share commentary on different topics. Some forums enable you as part of your message signature to include 'follow' hyperlinks to your web site. If you start posting in these types of forums, then each time your signature with the hyperlink appears is another chance for Google to index it and improve your site's ranking.

- **Twitter**

Twitter is a great SEO tool as you can include hyperlinks to your web site within your Twitter profile description. These links do count from an SEO perspective, and Google will index them. Furthermore, once you've created a Twitter account for your app, you can create profiles on Twitter-based services, such as Klout (http://www.klout.com) and Twellow (http://www.twellow.com), which also create profile pages based on your Twitter profile description. The net benefit from creating profiles with links to your website on all of these services is that you will gain a number of inbound links from high PR sites.

- **Web Directories**

Web directories are exactly what they sound like: categorized listings of websites. There are countless web directories online where you can submit your website's URL to be included. However, you should approach web directories with caution as the Google algorithm punishes lower-quality directories, which allow any web URL to be automatically accepted and posted. In general, you want to find free web directories that have some sort of approval mechanism before they accept a link. The presence of some sort of selectivity in the listings for a directory is recognized by Google and is extremely beneficial. Some popular web directories include Yahoo! Directory (http://dir.yahoo.com) and Dmoz (http://www.dmoz.org).

These are just a few starting points for initiating a link-building campaign for your app and website. Remember that the goal in link building is to get quality inbound links to your websites. Avoid the temptation to submit your link to sites that are spammy or are obviously constructed to game the Google algorithms. Google is on a constant mission to tweak their algorithm to punish these sites, so if your links are found on them, then your site's ranking will be negatively impacted.

SEM: Buying Advertising for Your App

While SEO deals with the process of improving your rankings in organic search results, SEM (Search Engine Marketing) is the process in which you pay for advertisements on Google. If you search for 'car insurance' on Google, you will notice sponsored results at the top of the search results for insurance companies like Allstate and Geico. When you click on one of these sponsored results, Google charges the company behind the link for that click. This is called Pay per Click (PPC) advertising and is at the heart of Google advertising. These insurance companies bid in a keyword auction that Google holds to have their advertisement displayed whenever users search for terms like 'car insurance' or 'insurance'. The company that bids the highest for these keywords is the one who's ad is displayed at the top. Anytime someone clicks on a sponsored link, the advertiser is charged for that click at whatever amount they had bid for that keyword.

Unless you are building a paid-download app, you should avoid SEM when marketing your app. The reason is quite simple: you are paying for that click and unless you have revenue you can obtain from the user who clicked on it, you will bleed cash. Furthermore, while using SEM to market your app will generate traffic to your site and increase downloads of your app, you aren't building an organic user base. If your goal is to have hundreds of thousands of users, the better way to get there is to build an app that is spread by the people who use it either through social media, word of mouth, or blog posts written about your app. An SEM campaign for a free app is a recipe to burn cash for limited long-term gain. In general, look to use SEM to promote your app only if you are able to potentially generate revenue from every person who clicks on a sponsored ad that lands at your app website.

9.5

Get Your App Reviewed

Be it restaurants, movies or apps, people love to rely on third-party reviews when contemplating a purchase decision. Given the vast number of apps that have entered the marketplace, app review sites have grown to play prominent role in the app marketing sphere. When your app is in a state where you feel comfortable having someone write a public review of it, you should reach out to any number of the app review sites that exist to try and get your app reviewed. In general, most app review sites allow developers of apps to submit their own apps for review, either for free or for a fixed price. When a review is written on your app, these review services give you the option to read it before it's released and choose to not release it if your app gets less than a favorable review.

App review sites generally come in two flavors: paid and free. While the notion of paying for a review of your app is ethically grey, it is a well-accepted way of getting attention directed towards your app. The truth is that most app sites receive so many free submissions from app developers that they do not have the bandwidth to process them all. Thus, most sites also offer different paid packages that include faster turnaround times and featured placement on their web sites. You should view app reviews as another promotional tool and invest some dollars in ensuring you get a few well-known app review sites write pieces on your app. Not only will these reviews generate buzz for your app, but the reviews they write will provide tangible SEO benefit if they include links back to your app web site.

Here are a few popular app review sites you can consider requesting a review for your app from:

148apps.com	Free
The iPhone App Review	Free + Paid ($39 - $270)
The Daily App Show	Paid ($55 - $280)
FreshApps	Paid ($100)

Figure 67: Different options for paid and unpaid app reviews

These are a few of the more well-known app review sites that have an open submission process. Getting your app reviewed by magazines and other web sites that do not accept developer submissions (like Gizmodo, Mashable, etc.) is a much tougher exercise. You will need to get in contact with app reviewers at each of those sites and find out what it takes to get your app featured on those sites.

Another type of app review sites are community based sites. These sites allow users to create profiles, and submit their own reviews of the apps they try. The most well-known of these social reviewing sites is Appolicious (http://www.appolicious.com). To get traction through these sites you will need people to write reviews on your apps. The best way to get traction on social reviewing sites is to leverage your network and get your friends and family to submit reviews of your app on these sites.

9.6

Use Press Releases

Press releases are a straightforward and effective way to build awareness of your app in the media. The benefits of using a press release to promote the launch of your app are twofold: it will increase the traffic to your app (as press releases are often syndicated on numerous popular news sites) and is a great way to build high-quality links back to your app and improve your SEO rankings.

A press release is a 500-800-word news report written to announce the launch of a new product, service or other noteworthy event. You do not need to be a reporter to write a press release. Anyone can do it. A press release is usually submitted to a single wire service, which then syndicates the release to numerous other news outlets on the Internet. It can cost anywhere from $50 - $400 to release a single article, depending on which press release service you use.

Figure 68: Sample press release for IdeaToAppster.com distributed through PRLog.org

The launch of your app is a great opportunity to write a press release that serves as a general announcement of the availability of your app. Once you've submitted your press release, other news editors, which syndicate content from wire services, can choose to display your press release prominently on their web site. Your news release can end up being syndicated by Google News, Yahoo News or any number of news web sites. We cannot understate the visibility your app will get from a well-written press release that is picked up by major tech news outlets. Your press release gives you an opportunity to introduce the world to your app and is a chance for you to generate organic buzz around it.

The SEO benefits of a press release are also noteworthy. A press release is a statement of text that can contain hyperlinks to anything you wish. A release written for an app should contain a few well-constructed hyperlinks back to your app's website in addition to its marketplace listing. When the press release is sent out, Google will index it and, depending on the quality of the press release service you use, you stand to benefit from the addition of a few, high-quality links pointing back to your website. Furthermore, these links will potentially be coming from highly-respected news websites, thus the SEO value of these inbound links will provide considerable bump to how Google views your app's website.

There are numerous press release sites on the Internet. You want to make sure you release on a service that provides syndication to high-quality news services, such as the Associated Press, Google News, Yahoo News, etc. Two popular press release services are: PR Web (http://www.prweb.com) and PR Log (http://www.prlog.org).

How to Write Effective Press Releases

The key to achieving good promotional and SEO success with a press release is writing engaging, impartial text that encourage news editors to feature your release on their web site. Press releases are meant to be news; hence, it's very important that it is written in the tone of a reporter covering your app's launch. Here are a few other important tips when writing a press release for your app:

- Create a 'hook' that compels readers to read beyond the headline and summary. Use the headline of your press release to the whet the appetite of your reader.
- Include pictures and videos in your release.
- It's ok to make expert-like statements in your press release about your app and the space it is in. Don't be afraid to sprinkle your text with statements about your app and how great it is.
- Avoid clichés.
- Use active voice in your writing. Use strong verbs in your text and do not write in a timid a fashion.

Structure of a Press Release

In general, press releases should follow a structure similar to this:

- **Headline**

A single line title for your press release. Your headline should be a short statement describing what you are announcing. In general, you should limit your headline to 60 characters. Use title case for your headlines. (Capitalize Every Word That is Longer Than Three Characters)

- **Summary**

One to four sentences that will appear below the headline and serve as a summary of what is contained in the full press release. You should keep your summary to less than 250 characters.

- **Body**

This is the meat of your release where you go into depth explaining your app and its launch. Don't be afraid to include both descriptive text along with quotes from interviews with yourself - and users! In general, your press release should be between 500 - 800 words. The body of your press release should begin with a dateline. The dateline is generally in the format of 'City, State, Day, Month, Year'. After the dateline comes the first line of your press release that should be a simple statement of the announcement you are making.

- **Boilerplate Contact Information**

At the end of your press release include a few sentences that describe your company, the people in it and any other important consideration to be given. This should also include a brief statement indicating whom to contact at your company for further information.

9.7

Going Viral: Every Appster's Dream

Going viral is the like getting discovered by the world, be it apps, memes, singers or actors. Viral marketing is a method of promotion that relies on people spreading word of your app through social media. The beauty of viral marketing is that if enough people continue to share word of your app then you can experience an exponential user growth curve. Viral marketing isn't something you pay for or have any control over; it happens on its own accord, it's free and you gain exposure to millions of users with no direct marketing expense.

However, building enough social media momentum to go viral is very difficult and ultimately depends on how interested people are in your app. Apps like DrawSomething and Instagram grew to their massive sizes primarily through viral spread of their app via Twitter and Facebook. The more people who used these apps, the more they talked about them in social media and the more other people would download and try them. What made Instagram that much more virally successful than competing apps like Hipstamatic? It's difficult to pinpoint exactly why, except to say that Instagram was built from the ground up with social media sharing as part of its feature set. Thus, the more people used Instagram and shared photos on Facebook and Twitter, the bigger its social media footprint grew, thus increasing its spread. Ultimately achieving viral marketing success depends on both making sure your app is appropriately plugged into social media channels in addition to your app actually being interesting.

In order to go viral, your app has to have the right integration with social media so that it gets visibility on social media sites like Twitter, attracts people's attention and provides an easy loop to convert them into users of your app. How well-positioned your app is to go viral will be defined by how well you create this social media loop. While going viral is a phenomenon that has no set recipe, here are some ways you can increase the chances that your app will go viral:

Allow users to share content from your app to their Facebook or Twitter feeds

Letting users share content they see in your app on their Twitter or Facebook feeds is a simple way to increase the social media footprint of your app. The more people share content from your app to social media, the more likely it is that non-users of your app who subscribe to these feeds might click on a shared link, see the content and have their interest piqued enough to download the app themselves. If we look at Dani's List, we can incorporate social media elements into its functionality by allowing users to share activities they find within the app to their Facebook and Twitter friends. This is a natural integration point for Dani's List, as it is likely that people would want to share an interesting activity they found with their family and friends. However, note that social media integration does require an app to have a publically-accessible website where non-users of the app can see what is being shared. In the case of Dani's List, we would need to create a web site that will display basic activity information to anyone who clicked on a link shared from the app. This does incur an additional engineering cost, however, developing a basic web site to display this information is well worth the cost to better position the app for viral growth.

Publish Events in Your App to the Facebook Activity Stream

Allowing users to share content from your app to Facebook still requires the user to push the 'share on Facebook' button, and this is something that many people are still hesitant to do. A deeper integration point to Facebook is to publish user actions within an app directly to their Facebook activity stream via Facebook's OpenGraph protocol. This differs from enabling people to share content to Facebook in that the user doesn't need to manually share items to Facebook. Instead, they are automatically posted by the app as they happen on their activity stream. The Facebook activity stream is visible to any of a user's friends and any item on it can be clicked to open up to a website with more details on the item.

Figure 69: Example an app publishing an action to a user's
Facebook Activity Stream

Deep integration into the Facebook activity stream requires
more thought and design than simply enabling users to share to
their Facebook wall. With the activity stream, you need to identify
the nouns and verbs in your app and then map them to actions and
objects that your app will publish to Facebook. The difference
between sharing something to Facebook and publishing to the
Facebook activity stream is that the latter posts content that is
structured in a way that Facebook can detect and provide a more
enhanced experience around. While this may sound
inconsequential, the benefit to you as an app builder is that by
publishing to the activity stream, Facebook can then automatically
build views on this (like monthly totals of user actions, awards
won, etc.) that will be visible on a user's Facebook profile.

App Name	Actions Published to Facebook	Objects Visible on Facebook
Spotify	"listened to" "created"	song playlist
Bahndr	"liked" "bahndred"	caption
Instagram	"added" "liked"	photo

Figure 70: How some apps integrate with the Facebook Activity
Stream

The Facebook Activity Stream is a great place to build awareness for your app. It requires no explicit action on the content creator's part, and immediately their action is visible to every one of their Facebook friends. Even if only one person actually clicks on the feed item, you'll still have generated a potential lead for someone to download and try your app. You can learn more about integrating your app into the Facebook activity stream by visiting http://developer.facebook.com.

If we turn our attention to Dani's List, we can expand the Facebook integration we introduced in the last chapter by publishing selected events within the app to a user's Facebook feed. There are three basic actions in Dani's List that make good candidates for publishing to the Facebook activity stream:

1. When a user **adds** a new **activity** to their what-to-do list.
2. When a user **completes** an **activity** on their what-to-do list.
3. When a user **creates** an **entirely** new activity.

Each of these actions might be interesting to other people on Facebook. The more of these actions that get published to Facebook, the greater the chance that a non-user of the app might click on one and decide to download and try the app. With each of the activities mentioned before, we would publish to Facebook a picture and text description of the activity so that within Facebook people would be able to see a preview of the action before clicking it and being directed to our website.

One thing to remember with the Facebook activity stream is user privacy. Not every user wants everything they do within an app to be broadcasted to all of their Facebook friends. At the very least, you need to include the ability for a user to enable or disable Facebook activity stream publishing in your app. A further step would be to turn off activity stream publishing by default and require users to enable it for the publishing to begin.

Allow users of your app to 'invite' non-users to join them in an activity

If you are creating a multiplayer app, a great way to give non-users a reason to download your app is to allow users of the app to start games/activities with them. Using Facebook or Twitter integration, your app can display a list of all of that users' friends and followers; from here, they can choose to start a game with any of them as though they were already users of the app. If the user chooses someone who is not a user of the app, but merely a Facebook friend, you can create an 'invite' within Facebook for the person to join. This invite is posted on the friend's Facebook wall and can say something like, "Your friend Herb wants you to join them playing X, a cool new iPhone game." Once this new user accepts Herb's invite, they can then immediately start interacting with the person who invited them within the app. This is another powerful way to increase virality as users are given a very compelling reason to download the app. Behavioral economics teaches that 'social pressure' is a powerful motivating force in buying decisions. By delivering invites directly from friends already in the app to those who aren't, people are given a very strong nudge to also become users themselves.

Create a closed invite-only program for accepting new users

Paradoxically, if you close off your app from allowing anybody to join, you can leverage another behavioral economic concept, exclusivity, to cultivate demand for your app. Google pioneered this method in 2004 when it introduced its Gmail product. Each initial user of Gmail was given a small number of invites to the app they could distribute to their friends at will. Every user who received an invitation and joined Gmail then received X more invites to distribute to their friends. This type of closed invitation model relies on user's interest to be piqued by the thought of a new service that they cannot join. If the users who are on your app generate enough social media buzz about it and spread their invitations, then demand for invitations will sky rocket.

To tap into this demand you can create an email address submission form on a website where users who aren't on the app can request an invitation. After submitting their email address, the web site would display something akin to, "We will contact you when a spot has opened up for you on X." Regardless if there is any capacity constraint within your app, you should wait a few days and then send out invitations to the users who had previously registered, informing them that, "We've expanded our beta program and you are now welcome to join." This second email would contain a link to directly sign the user up to the app and download it.

While this closed invitation system sounds somewhat pretentious and needless, do not discount the psychological factors in play when people see invites to services that their friends are using. If you are able to create the necessary buzz around the invitations, you'll find the closed invitation model will result in an overload of user's wanting to be put on a waiting list to use your app.

Market your app through social bookmarking services like Reddit, Delicious

If you have clicked on a link that opened to a picture of cat pining for a cheeseburger, then you've probably seen a *meme*. Memes are funny (supposedly) or entertaining links to pictures or videos that go viral and achieve pop culture notoriety doing so. Much of modern meme culture stems from social link sharing sites, such as Reddit. For those who've never heard of Reddit, it is a website where users across the world share links which other users can 'up-vote' or 'down-vote.' The end result of Reddit is that entertaining content bubbles its way to the top as they receive the most number of 'up-votes.' Reddit is one of the most popular web sites in the world (having an Alexa rating of #123 in July 2012), and is commonly identified as the originating source for many of the memes and other viral content that emerges.

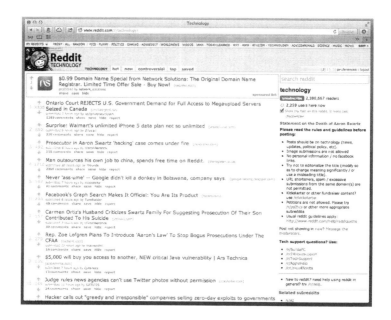

Figure 71: Links shared on Reddit's Technology list

If you are building an app that generates content, like a photo-sharing or a social-curation concept, then look at Reddit as a potential vehicle to fuel growth of your app through traffic to your website. The hope of this strategy is to post content from your app on Reddit so that it generates enough up-votes that more and more Redditors (that's what people who use Reddit are known as) see it, click on it and potentially download your app. If the content you create is funny, or interesting enough, it has the potential to rocket to the front-page of Reddit, a veritable gold mine of free traffic to your website if you can achieve it. Much like how you'd convert someone clicking on a link on Facebook, you can use advertising on the webpage to entice users to try your app.

If you app isn't one that generates content that can be shared on Reddit, you can still use the site to generate buzz around your app itself. Reddit is composed of hundreds of thousands of 'subreddits,' which are sub-forums focusing one particular topic or area. There are hundreds of subreddits dedicated to sharing the latest app releases and news surrounding the smartphone ecosystem. By making a concerted effort to create and share links about your app on Reddit, you can achieve the same effect as having content created by your app shared on Reddit.

As we reach the end of this chapter, you should understand that great apps aren't just a product of what the app does, or how it looks. Just like the world of physical goods, creating a great product requires creating a story that you can tell your prospective customers. As you progress through the phases of creating an app, don't let yourself be lulled into the belief that your app will attract a rush of users to it by virtue of its own credentials. The marketplaces have hundreds of thousands of apps within them and if you do not spend the effort to market your app to the public and create awareness of what it does, it's likely to get lost amidst the crowd. Start your marketing planning early in your development process and cultivate awareness for your app as it moves from planning to beta to final release. Use the web to build a following for your app long before it is ever released and leverage social media as a free and effective tool to build awareness. Ultimately, your goal should be to have enough interest built in your app that by the time you release it on the marketplace, there is a waiting tide of people to try it, talk about it and share it with their friends.

10

Conclusion: The Road Ahead

You made it! In case the name of this chapter didn't tip you off, we are nearing the end of our journey together. Over the course of this book we've tried to outline all the major aspects of building your own mobile app, from testing your idea to designing your app; from managing a development team to marketing your released app; and a whole lot in between. Our aim was not to teach you how to code, but rather to illuminate the path from having just an idea to becoming an Appster. If you are to take one thing from this book, let it be the 10 Appster Commandments. If you haven't already, print these out and tape them somewhere where you can see them every day:

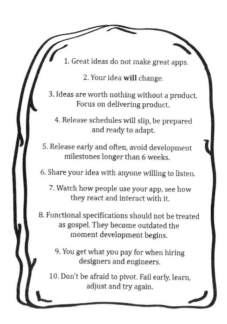

1. Great ideas do not make great apps.

2. Your idea **will** change.

3. Ideas are worth nothing without a product. Focus on delivering product.

4. Release schedules will slip, be prepared and ready to adapt.

5. Release early and often, avoid development milestones longer than 6 weeks.

6. Share your idea with anyone willing to listen.

7. Watch how people use your app, see how they react and interact with it.

8. Functional specifications should not be treated as gospel. They become outdated the moment development begins.

9. You get what you pay for when hiring designers and engineers.

10. Don't be afraid to pivot. Fail early, learn, adjust and try again.

Figure 72: Remember these commandments as your embark on building your app

With these commandments to guide you and equipped with the knowledge contained within this book, you are ready to move forward and turn your idea into a mobile app. Remember, ideas by themselves are worth very little, and there is little use spinning in circles waiting for the perfect idea to pop into your head. Even if you have only a half-baked notion of what you want your app to do, it's still worth the time and effort to take the next steps and start bringing it to life. Your idea will evolve and change, and might end up becoming something completely different. The funny thing about apps is that the really amazing ideas often turn out to be duds, and the weird and dull-sounding often end up being smash successes. Even in the worst case where your app is not successful, just by going through the process of bringing an app to the market you would have learned a foundational set of entrepreneurial and technical knowledge that will make your next idea that much more likely to succeed.

The road to becoming an Appster is long and curvy with no guarantee you won't end up going in a few circles along the way. When it comes to apps, failure isn't a reason for you to give up. Far from it, failure is a necessary step in the evolution of your app. Instagram initially started out named 'Burbn' and was originally meant to be an app like Foursquare. Only after building the first version and seeing that it didn't work like they imagined did the founders pivot to land on the idea for Instagram. Rarely do the great apps emerge in the first version. They are instead the product of an evolution of ideas and trials that lead to a breakout moment.

We are the dawn of an entirely new era of computing, with mobile apps being at the vanguard of the post-PC mode of computing. Even with 800,000+ apps in the Apple App Store, the era of the app is just beginning. A cursory look at our lives reveal many areas where apps have yet to leave their mark, from world-changing opportunities in mobile payments all the way down to just knowing what music people around you are listening to. In 2007, the app had just begun to upend all our notions of what a smartphone should be. In 2010, the app jumped from the smartphone to the tablet and brought with it another computing revolution. In 2012, apps are again poised to make another jump as they begin to revolutionize the way we interact with our TVs and consume media at home. Looking ahead, the potential for apps to transform our lives is limitless. From the automobiles in our garage to the appliances in our kitchen, apps are poised to open new frontiers of computing that will continue to revolutionize the way we interact with each other and the world.

So what are you waiting for? If you have an idea, and you want to turn it into an app, do not let a lack of technical knowledge, time or confidence hold you back. We've given you most of the information you need to start down the road to launching your own app. All that's left is for you to take the next step and put this knowledge to work. We stand at a once in a generation moment and you have the opportunity to be at the vanguard of an entirely new way of consuming technology. Even in the worst case, what do you have to lose besides your time and some money? The upside is potentially limitless - and will remain unknown until you try.

As our text ends and you embark on your own journey to becoming an Appster, remember this quote from the wisdom of Mark Twain:

"Twenty years from now you will be more disappointed by the things that you didn't do than by the ones you did do. So throw off the bowlines. Sail away from the safe harbor. Catch the trade winds in your sails. Explore. Dream. Discover."

— Mark Twain

About the Authors

Bobby Gill

Bobby Gill is the founder of Blue Label Labs, a mobile app development lab based in New York and Seattle. Blue Label Labs has released several apps for Android, iOS and Windows Phone. In addition to their own apps, Blue Label Labs provides design and engineering services to mobile app clients across the world. Prior to starting Blue Label Labs, Bobby spent 4 years at Microsoft as a Program Manager within the Forefront Identity Manager (FIM) product group. During this time, Bobby served as an engineering and architectural lead for the FIM server specializing in database and web service design. After Microsoft, Bobby worked as a Summer Associate at McKinsey & Co. where he was part of a service operations enhancement program within the high-tech industry. Bobby holds a Bachelor of Mathematics specializing in Computer Science from the University of Waterloo and a Masters in Business Administration from Columbia Business School.

Jordan Gurrieri

Jordan Gurrieri, founder of Blue Label Labs, is the lead product designer and front-end developer at the development lab. Prior to Blue Label, Jordan spent 6 years working in a variety of roles within Microsoft. During his tenure, Jordan acted as a business process and systems engineer, developing line of business applications to support operational and growth activities across the company's international subsidiaries. In his later years, he served as Senior Product Manager for Windows consumer products, then including Hotmail, Messenger and SkyDrive cloud apps. Jordan graduated from the University of Toronto with a Bachelor of Applied Science in Computer & Electrical Engineering.

References

1. http://tech.fortune.cnn.com/2011/11/21/piper-jaffray-android-app-revenue-is-7-of-iphones/
2. http://www.forbes.com/sites/toddhixon/2011/12/15/the-post-pc-era-starts-to-make-sense/
3. http://en.wikipedia.org/wiki/Android_(operating_system)#Market_share
4. http://parislemon.com/post/16997124721/size-matters
5. http://www.bgr.com/2012/09/28/ios-android-market-share-grows/
6. http://mashable.com/2012/11/01/google-apps-tie-apple/
7. http://paidcontent.org/2011/08/30/419-apple-has-finally-pulled-financial-times-from-ios/
8. http://mashable.com/2011/02/01/apps-used-once/
9. http://www.forbes.com/sites/insertcoin/2012/05/04/draw-something-loses-5m-users-a-month-after-zynga-purchase/
10. http://www.quora.com/Instagram/How-many-users-does-Instagram-have
11. http://www.geekwire.com/2011/number-reason-startups-fail-premature-scaling/
12. http://www.forbes.com/sites/bruceupbin/2012/04/09/facebook-buys-instagram-for-1-billion-wheres-the-revenue/
13. http://www.padgadget.com/2012/01/17/freemium-apps-predicted-to-be-the-biggest-market-in-the-app-store/
14. http://www.gartner.com/it/page.jsp?id=2017015
15. http://tech.fortune.cnn.com/2011/11/21/piper-jaffray-android-app-revenue-is-7-of-iphones/
16. http://www.businessinsider.com/chart-of-the-day-the-app-economy-is-35-billion-2012-6
17. http://tech.fortune.cnn.com/2011/11/21/piper-jaffray-android-app-revenue-is-7-of-iphones/
18. http://www.idc.com/getdoc.jsp?containerId=prUS23818212#.UPDzFKWLFur
19. http://www.pcmag.com/article2/0,2817,2411372,00.asp
20. http://www.14oranges.com/2012/11/ios-version-

statistics-—-novembe-14th-2012/
21. https://developer.apple.com/appstore/resources/approva
l/guidelines.html
22. http://www.bis.doc.gov/encryption/question3_sub.htm
23. http://techcrunch.com/2012/10/25/in-mobile-ads-ios-is-
still-the-most-valuable-platform-apps-drive-73-of-all-
revenues-says-opera/
24. http://www.appbrain.com/stats/top-android-sdk-version

25670989R00134

Printed in Great Britain
by Amazon